LETTERS TO DAVID

An older man writes letters to himself,
as a younger man, on critical areas of living

DAVID K WEBB MD

Cover design by Liza Wynette

"To all those who desire God's wisdom and seek to walk in it"

Table of Contents

Introduction

Proverbs 1:7 "The fear of the Lord is the beginning of knowledge, but fools despise wisdom and discipline."

Wisdom is a precious gem that should be sought by all and shared by those who possess it. Wisdom can be thought of as knowledge that is applied to daily living. It has its origin in a restored relationship with God that then allows His Spirit to transform us to be able to live as He intended for us to live. Although not the exclusive possession of the "aged," the years of living in this world provides opportunity to "test and approve…." (Romans 12:2) godly wisdom.

Some years ago, I was reading a book by a godly man who made the statement: "…. I wish that I had known at age 25 what I now understand."[1] Although he was referring to the issue of the Church, I wondered if that same thought could be expanded to other areas of life. I felt led then to write, as a 72-year-old man, letters to myself, when I was age 30. I wanted to convey what I had learned about selected issues of life to my hypothetical self as a young man so that I could perhaps employ these understandings in my life going forward. Obviously, I cannot go back in time and relive these years, but I wonder if there are other younger people who might, armed with some insights, find benefit as they live out the rest of their adult lives.

I do not claim to have properly lived the areas I write about; I would claim to have made proper choices in a few areas, but I fell short or failed to various degrees in other areas. Some areas I really never considered or constructively regarded and therefore missed the opportunities to address them. "Rebuke" is a word rarely used in everyday language – it has a sharp and critical tone to it. Yet if understood properly it conveys the heart of what I am seeking to accomplish with this book. Rebuke should be understood as a challenge that leads to reconsideration that then could bring a redirection or reconstruction of how one lives some aspect of their life.

My goal with this book is not to influence the reader to agree with me and to comply with my exhortations and admonishments, but that they be rebuked: challenged to seriously regard the issues I surface. By doing this I hope that each person will come to an intentional and thoughtful approach on given topics so that they will live life more wisely than I have.

I have linked the topics with Biblical references since these, in my view, are the source of true knowledge. Those references are only a few that could be quoted but will serve the reader as a beginning point for further study. I have also added at the end of each letter a brief "study guide" that is intended to facilitate the reader, in discussion perhaps with others, to truly confront the issue and develop their own strategy to address it.

There may be other topics that arise in your mind that I have not addressed; these are only those that I have come to feel are important and for which I have in many cases been inadequately or poorly prepared to address. I encourage the reader to expand the topics to include those that come to their awareness.

Enjoy and be challenged by "Letters to David."

[1]Letters to the Church: by Francis Chan

Part 1
Personal Development

Will
Letter 1

Mark 8:34-37
³⁴ Then he called the crowd to him along with his disciples and said: "Whoever wants to be my disciple must deny themselves and take up their cross and follow me. ³⁵ For whoever wants to save their life will lose it, but whoever loses their life for me and for the gospel will save it. ³⁶ What good is it for someone to gain the whole world, yet forfeit their soul? ³⁷ Or what can anyone give in exchange for their soul?

Ephesians 5:17
¹⁷ Take the helmet of salvation and the sword of the Spirit, which is the word of God.

Colossians 1:9
⁹ For this reason, since the day we heard about you, we have not stopped praying for you. We continually ask God to fill you with the knowledge of his will through all the wisdom and understanding that the Spirit gives.

Dear David,

I want, in this letter, to address a fundamental issue that must be acknowledged, understood and a decision upon it made. To do so at your age now is already later in your life than ideal, but it is important for the rest of your years that it be dealt with even at this point. The world and our society teach and demonstrate living a life for self; it rewards those who do so. Our fallen flesh nature urges us on in this direction. We take pride (a word that speaks volumes) in our ability to determine and accomplish "what I want, what makes me happy, what brings me wealth and position, what causes people to praise me and what gives me control of my life." <u>Our</u> will is in control of our whole being and we build our priorities, goals, choices and interactions around this will; everything we think, feel, speak and do must be brought to align with <u>our</u> will. Those who interfere with, or present obstacles to, this orientation are certain to be rejected or removed from our presence. <u>Our</u> will is the god that rules and directs our life.

This is the underlying and unchallenged orientation of all mankind, and it has risen to its highest perfection in our modern Western culture. Our computer driven technology of today, such as social media, texting and instant gratification methods (e.g.: "Amazon Prime") focuses our lives on "me and my will." Such technology breeds a life style and sterile communication methods which promote individualism, self-centeredness, isolation, loneliness and entitlement. It opposes personal interactions within family and community; it depersonalizes society. In short, we are being led and influenced further and further away from the relational, moral, community-focused people we were created to be. We were (and are) made in God's image and this pride fueled, self-focused existence is counter and destructive to the people we were created to be.

The critical decision you must address is: whose will do you choose to allow to determine your life's course? Standing apart from and often counter to our individualistic human will is the "good, pleasing and perfect" will of God (Romans 12:2). His will alone knows, understands and coordinates all of creation so that as we choose to live according to His will, we are able to live life fully and know an inner satisfaction that can never be realized in any other way. You, like every person, have a choice: you can choose to know His will for you individually as it resides within His larger will for all of creation, or you can seek to follow your own self-seeking will that will frequently place you in opposition to Him and His greater and better will. You must understand that if you choose the latter you will lose; you will never know true joy and peace.

Our flesh, the world, and society (all directed and ruled by the "enemy" – Satan) tell us that pleasure and happiness are found by seeking your own self-will and doing whatever it takes to build your own empire, with you as king. The truth is, though, that following this course will only bring personal destruction, unhealthy and failed relationships and death. This death is not the physical death of our human body (of which all humans will face) but the death, while physically alive, of your inner self and eternal death after this life is over. One will only know joy, peace and fulfillment as they meld their individual wills with that of God's; their true identity will be discovered, and their purpose realized as they progressively grow to know and submit to Him more and more.

But to be candid, David, this will not be easy, and you will feel at times that you are depriving yourself of the glitz and glamor of worldly pleasures. You will be subtly and perhaps openly criticized by the main stream of society; you may be scorned, mocked and belittled because you represent that which implicitly judges the world's standards and goals. Yet you must hold fast to what is truth for your benefit, as well as for your children's and for your grandchildren's benefit. The choice of whose will you allow to direct your life will impact and be powerfully important to the succeeding generations.

Convince yourself of the importance of this decision; talk with those older who reflect true joy and peace in their life, study God's Word (especially the life and teachings of Christ) and pray for understanding and direction. Then, with courage and determination, live your life fully and completely in His will. Never look back for your reward will be great.

Love,
David

Questions

Obviously in normal life one does not have the advantage to be able to evaluate and direct their life choices with the knowledge of their future. However, the author has in these letters created such a context to press each of us to focus on specific "life issues" proactively and intentionally in our younger years so that we, as we go forward, can direct our lives toward the best of all outcomes. These general questions should be regarded as a guide for the reader, individually or as a part of a small group, to address the issue at hand and make appropriate life decisions and choices.

What is the specific "life issue" the author is concerned about in this letter?

Why does the author feel this is an important issue to bring to a person's attention in their younger years; do you agree?

How did the author seem to deal with it as a younger man? Was his means of addressing the issue done properly or improperly, consciously or subconsciously, constructively or destructively, God honoring or man honoring?

How is the author, now as an older man, recommending that the specific issue be thought about and actively addressed?

The goal of each letter is not to convince the reader to deal with the issue as the author had, but to embrace the issue and determine for themselves how they choose to regard and deal with it in their lives.

Do you agree with the author's analyses and recommended manner of addressing it?

If so, explain how you will apply it in your specific life's circumstances.

If not, please elaborate on how you view the issue and how you plan to address it as you live out the rest of your life.

What wisdom would you desire your children to receive from you on this issue to better prepare and equip them to deal with it in a truthful and God-honoring manner?

Integrity
Letter 2

[22] You were taught, with regard to your former way of life, to put off your old self, which is being corrupted by its deceitful desires; [23] to be made new in the attitude of your minds; [24] and to put on the new self, created to be like God in true righteousness and holiness.

[25] Therefore each of you must put off falsehood and speak truthfully to your neighbor, for we are all members of one body. [26] "In your anger do not sin": Do not let the sun go down while you are still angry, [27] and do not give the devil a foothold. [28] Anyone who has been stealing must steal no longer, but must work, doing something useful with their own hands, that they may have something to share with those in need.

[29] Do not let any unwholesome talk come out of your mouths, but only what is helpful for building others up according to their needs, that it may benefit those who listen. [30] And do not grieve the Holy Spirit of God, with whom you were sealed for the day of redemption. [31] Get rid of all bitterness, rage and anger, brawling and slander, along with every form of malice. [32] Be kind and compassionate ; forgiving each other, just as in Christ God forgave your 5:1 erefore, as dearly loved children [2] and walk in the u gave himself up for us as a fragrant offering and sacri

Dear David,

If you are not grounding y New Creation in Christ," then you will adopt and reflect ties of this world. These qualities are rooted in the fou edness. The philosophy of the world that influences a tever you need to do to get ahead and secure wealth ment is the accepted evidence of worldly success. Ii people push the limits of civil law and are willing to violate what moral consciousness defines as "right and wrong." Sadly, this has resulted in a society where the character qualities God intended for His human creation have been disregarded or have become self-serving. Therefore, in order to live as God intended, as a new creation, you will need to intentionally differentiate yourself from the world.

With this reality in mind I want to bring to your attention that which I have come to believe is the one quality that best summarizes Christian Character: Integrity. This quality should pervade the very fabric of your being and powerfully influence the various aspects of your life. It should serve as an internal directive and check on your thought life, motives, priorities and decisions. It should govern how you use your time and how you deal with the temptations of the flesh that seek to invade and destroy your life. It should define your relationships and your role as a husband, father, and physician. Integrity should determine the words you speak and how you speak them; it should direct every act, large and small. A person of integrity is one whose inner person is identical to that outer person whose words and behavior are observed by the world; the inner defines and directs a person's outward manifestations.

Integrity can be broken down into several more easily understood and applicable sub-qualities. These sub-qualities can also be viewed as fruits that are produced from the root of integrity. The first of these is honesty and dependability, two features that are linked together. A person must speak only what they can validate as truth; they should never allow lying or misrepresentation to be part of their character. Further, a person must hold themselves accountable to do what they say and be relied upon to do it in the time and manner they have so committed. Sadly, our fallen world acts in a way that reflects a philosophy that a person's word cannot be relied upon as truthful and is just an intent or a suggestion and not a guarantee of their conduct. We have lowered our expectations of people to such an extent that we are surprised and suspicious when one acts honestly and dependably.

The second sub-quality or fruit of integrity is the acquisition of sufficient and proper knowledge that then directs one's actions according to what he or she understands as truth. Wisdom is the practical application of knowledge in daily life. The life of a person of integrity should, in every detail, be lived out predictably and consistently according to their embraced understanding of truth. For you, the Bible defines a solid, universally applicable knowledge base; applying its truth in you daily life will result in a fruitful and satisfying life.

Words, as the scripture repeatedly admonishes, are a "picture window" to our true character. The proper and beneficial use of words represent a third sub-quality of integrity. A person of integrity holds themselves to a high standard relative to what they speak, how they speak and even when they speak. Words should reflect our God-grounded world-view and our inner recreated person; they must align themselves with our identity in Christ. Words are an important and powerful instrument that affects others and can be constructive and life-giving or destructive and life-taking. Words are the most powerful of all human relational resources. We must carefully choose our words sensitively; even before we utter them, we must be sure that they will be pleasing to God. I often seek to hear from the Holy Spirit the very words that my tongue forms.

As a fourth sub-quality, a person of integrity must be able to recognize the brokenness of the world and the great need of others around them. Such recognition should then demand obedient action. Building our integrity upon a biblical world view will allow us to know and adopt God's heart of justice for the suffering and the plight of those oppressed and poor in our midst. I believe God places in our view those He wants us to help (in a variety of ways), but you must keep your eyes and ears open to His leading. Integrity demands a sensitivity toward and willingness to act in and with justice.

Perseverance is a fifth sub-quality of a person of integrity. Paul, Peter and James all hold perseverance high as an important aspect of Christian character and as a powerful means to grow in spiritual maturity (See Romans 5:3-5; 1 Peter 1:6-7; James 1:2-4). The world allows and encourages us to be weak in this quality; it expects us to not complete what we begin. When life gets hard or is not at that moment giving pleasure or happiness, then the world teaches that it is acceptable to give up and try something else. Society also endorses that it is fine to accept less than what you are capable and to give less than your full effort. The quality of perseverance should modify and empower ones use of their time, opportunities and skills in order to accomplish completely and with excellence what a person has previously determine to be God's will for them. Integrity breeds and expects perseverance.

As the final sub-quality or fruit, a person of integrity should have a proper and humbly high view of themselves; they should regard themselves as confident, strong and secure. This positive view of oneself is necessary to be able to withstand the resistance and counter efforts of the world as one serves God according to His calling. Yet the person of integrity is fully aware that this proper view of themselves is only possible with and flows out of an intimate and growing relationship with God. They can avoid being prideful or self-exalting because they are continually aware that apart from Christ, they are nothing and can do nothing that is valuable.

Integrity, David, is the highest of Christian character traits – seek this for your life and instill it into the lives of your children and grandchildren. In this you will reflect the person of our Lord and Savior.

Love,
David.

Questions

Obviously in normal life one does not have the advantage to be able to evaluate and direct their life choices with the knowledge of their future. However, the author has in these letters created such a context to press each of us to focus on specific "life issues" proactively and intentionally in our younger years so that we, as we go forward, can direct our lives toward the best of all outcomes. These general questions should be regarded as a guide for the reader, individually or as a part of a small group, to address the issue at hand and make appropriate life decisions and choices.

What is the specific "life issue" the author is concerned about in this letter?

Why does the author feel this is an important issue to bring to a person's attention in their younger years; do you agree?

How did the author seem to deal with it as a younger man? Was his means of addressing the issue done properly or improperly, consciously or subconsciously, constructively or destructively, God honoring or man honoring?

How is the author, now as an older man, recommending that the specific issue be thought about and actively addressed?

The goal of each letter is not to convince the reader to deal with the issue as the author had, but to embrace the issue and determine for themselves how they choose to regard and deal with it in their lives.

Do you agree with the author's analyses and recommended manner of addressing it?

If so, explain how you will apply it in your specific life's circumstances.

If not, please elaborate on how you view the issue and how you plan to address it as you live out the rest of your life.

What wisdom would you desire your children to receive from you on this issue to better prepare and equip them to deal with it in a truthful and God-honoring manner?

Listening
Letter 3

Ephesians 4:15-16; 29

15 Instead, speaking the truth in love, we will grow to become in every respect the mature body of him who is the head, that is, Christ. 16 From him the whole body, joined and held together by every supporting ligament, grows and builds itself up in love, as each part does its work.

29 Do not let any unwholesome talk come out of your mouths, but only what is helpful for building others up according to their needs, that it may benefit those who listen.

James 1:9

9 Believers in humble circumstances ought to take pride in their high position.

Dear David,

By this time in your life you have become aware of, and frustrated by, an unexpected reality – the reality that people are poor listeners. You have, and will continue to, become increasingly aware that people do not either desire to listen to another, or have never been taught, or modeled, proper "active listening." I believe this stems from and is symptomatic of our self-centered and a "me-focused" world view, which is, of course, a manifestation of the foundational sin of pride.

As an example, it is disheartening and discouraging to you and Judy that when you invite a couple or two to your home for dinner and an evening of fellowship, that the conversation seems to generally focus only on them and their world. They rarely ask you questions or seem interested in you or your lives. They seem happy and gratified that you listen actively to them portray their lives yet don't seem to care about knowing you. You have wondered if it was because you were viewed by them as being socially "higher", so they felt a bit intimidated, or maybe they regarded you as just not that interesting. You will discover, as time goes on, that this will happen repeatedly and in many other life situations. Simply stated, people generally just cannot get out of themselves long enough to want to consider another person. Additionally, even if people seek to know another at a deeper level, many do not know or have not been taught how to properly listen relationally. The result then is that one is discouraged from attempting to build relationships and develop good friendships. Ultimately this outcome is very harmful and counterproductive to the goal of using our lives to be a testimony for Christ. If we don't spend time with others and get to know them deeply, they will be less likely to see and be attracted to the Christ that lives in us! Satan often uses isolation and separation to retard the building of the Kingdom of God. The original sin of pride has damaged people's ability to develop relationships that could strengthen and edify one another and allow His spiritual "light" to be in view to another.

People want to be heard and known by others but do not desire to know another, reflecting their unspoken and deeply rooted desire for self-exaltation. It's important that you understand this and examine yourself so that this prideful motivation is not active in you as you develop deeper relationships with others. When you share yourself with others, scrutinize what you choose to share so its purpose is not to bring yourself glory. Be sure what you share and reveal is also honest and balanced; be willing to be vulnerable and real in the presence of others. This, by the way, will give them permission to be the same in your presence.

You must strive to be a "good listener" – active, intentional and sincere. It requires practice and self-discipline. It is not only essential to non-family social relationships but is critical to a good marriage and the proper nurturing of your children. It is also key to being successful in one's work, in your case as a Family Physician. Listening, properly done, is both verbal and nonverbal. Really trying to understand and know a person requires insightful questioning and reflective statements that show them that you "hear them," that you are "on the same page they are on" and that you are empathetic to their communication. Do not confuse sympathy with empathy; sympathy can be expressed when appropriate to a given situation, such as in the expression of sadness or grief, but empathy can be part of all conversations. It simply requires that you, as much as possible, see and feel life from the others' perspective. When a person feels they are being heard empathetically they will feel energized, cared about, secure and satisfied at a deep soul level. They will be encouraged to continue to be more open, honest and vulnerable; you will be viewed as trustworthy and safe.

Nonverbal interactions are very powerful in this process of active listening. Eye contact, body posture and avoidance of distractions all convey to the other: "I am really interested in you." The fastest way to shut down deep sharing is to glance (even for a second) at your cell phone or to be peeking out the window while another person is talking. There are many potential distractions in our modern world that can invade our relational encounter. In our fast-paced world people pride themselves on being able to "multi-task;" if they do this while in a listening posture, they will be viewed as disinterested or that the person speaking is not valuable. Proper listening is so uncommon in this age that when we do really listen, the person before us is surprised and powerfully impressed.

Don't be afraid to hear things that may surprise, annoy, or sadden you. What is shared or revealed also may cause you to have to re-evaluate how you have related to that person in the past. If you have, for instance, offended them in some way, hearing them properly may require you to seek their forgiveness and to work together to build a better relationship. What they reveal may change how you now regard them compared to previously; your interaction together from that point on may not be the same as before. But no matter what is heard or how you are affected by it, it will draw you both into a deeper, more honest and committed relationship.

Active listening brings an enhanced depth of inner joy and peace. We were created for deep intimacy and fellowship with God and with other people. When we, even for an evening, return to this created intent we are experiencing what is God's desire and intended blessing for us.

David, learn and practice true listening at all levels of your life, in all types of circumstances and with those God places in your life. Be guided by His Spirit and be willing to "hear another person." Your life will be richer and your impact upon others more powerful as you seek to know them and be known by them.

Love,
David

Questions

Obviously in normal life one does not have the advantage to be able to evaluate and direct their life choices with the knowledge of their future. However, the author has in these letters created such a context to press each of us to focus on specific "life issues" proactively and intentionally in our younger years so that we, as we go forward, can direct our lives toward the best of all outcomes. These general questions should be regarded as a guide for the reader, individually or as a part of a small group, to address the issue at hand and make appropriate life decisions and choices.

What is the specific "life issue" the author is concerned about in this letter?

Why does the author feel this is an important issue to bring to a person's attention in their younger years; do you agree?

How did the author seem to deal with it as a younger man? Was his means of addressing the issue done properly or improperly, consciously or subconsciously, constructively or destructively, God honoring or man honoring?

How is the author, now as an older man, recommending that the specific issue be thought about and actively addressed?

The goal of each letter is not to convince the reader to deal with the issue as the author had, but to embrace the issue and determine for themselves how they choose to regard and deal with it in their lives.

Do you agree with the author's analyses and recommended manner of addressing it?

If so, explain how you will apply it in your specific life's circumstances.

If not, please elaborate on how you view the issue and how you plan to address it as you live out the rest of your life.

What wisdom would you desire your children to receive from you on this issue to better prepare and equip them to deal with it in a truthful and God-honoring manner?

Worry
Letter 4

Matthew 6:25-27
²⁵ "Therefore I tell you, do not worry about your life, what you will eat or drink; or about your body, what you will wear. Is not life more than food, and the body more than clothes? ²⁶ Look at the birds of the air; they do not sow or reap or store away in barns, and yet your heavenly Father feeds them. Are you not much more valuable than they? ²⁷ Can any one of you by worrying add a single hour to your life?

³³ But seek first his kingdom and his righteousness, and all these things will be given to you as well.

1 Peter 5:7
⁷ Cast all your anxiety on him because he cares for you.

Romans 8:15
¹⁵ The Spirit you received does not make you slaves, so that you live in fear again; rather, the Spirit you received brought about your adoption to sonship. And by him we cry, "Abba, Father."

Dear David,

Recently I have been studying the Gospel of Luke. In Chapter 12 Jesus is telling His disciples and those who have gathered around Him to not be anxious or worried about the day-by-day provisions for life. He points to other parts of His creation: the raven, the lilies, and the grass, as examples of how God, the creator, cares for His creation. They do not concern themselves, even in the least, with making themselves into what they were created to be or even how long they would live in this world – these things are not in their control or even a part of their awareness. They don't stress, worry or fret about their existence. Jesus then points out that if God loves and provides for these parts of His creation, would He not care just as well for the pinnacle of His creation: mankind.

Before the fall, God provided everything in fullness and perfection; He walked with His human creation in intimate fellowship. Man was created in His image and was to represent Him as His royal delegate in this created world, to have dominion over all other aspects of creation. This role of domination, however, was not oppressive or conflictual; it was mutually pleasing and faciliatory to all aspects of the creation. However, with the fall, when man sought to be his own god, a new reality entered the world with man now separated from God's fellowship. Man had to exist and labor now in an oppositional and a harm-intending world; now for the first time he experienced fear, worry and anxiety. In addition, man, now viewing himself as his own god, in an effort to reduce fear and conflict, sought to control his life and environment. He came to rely upon his own resources and limited wisdom to protect himself. In accordance with the ways of the fallen world he sought to accumulate wealth and material possessions and to rise in his societal position in an effort to hold and yield power. However, the more possessions he accumulated and the higher his position in society became, the more he worried about protecting and holding onto this hollow self-generated kingdom. The God-created man now walks in fear; seeing the rest of the world as a potential and unpredictable threat to this fragile human state.

Jesus teaches us the key to be able to live a life of progressively decreasing worry, anxiety and fear. The key is found in Luke 12:3: we are to "seek first the Kingdom of God...."! As we place this as our number one priority then God has promised that He will provide all we need (as opposed to "want") for life. The life He will provide for each of us will be according to His will (His good, perfect, pleasing will: Romans 12:2) but this will at times involve some degree of human discomfort. Often His will for our lives may not be accomplished in the time frame we, in our humanness, desire. Frequently His will is not understandable or rational to our human mind. You must resolve to trust Him as the sovereign, all-wise God. Although the life he gives will render true peace and joy and provide what is essential for existence, He doesn't promise to give the things the world promotes. At times He will bless His children with worldly happiness and material things to satisfy their flesh desires but that is His choice and according to His infinitely wise will. As we enjoy these God granted worldly pleasures, we must, however, be careful. If we lose focus and begin to slide back into the world's ways of thinking and living, He loves us enough to strongly intervene in order to guard and protect us from the destructive ways of the world.

To seek first the Kingdom of God and depend on Him to provide what you need is counter-cultural: it will be viewed as radical and a societal-opposing world-view. It will be regarded as judgmental to the philosophies and ways of the fallen world; you will feel like you are an alien and a stranger to the culture's norm. The world may truly be unkind to you and make your efforts difficult. Additionally, to live with victory over worry requires you to "seek" His Kingdom. Seeking means to be intentional, proactive, goal oriented and undaunted in an effort to secure or arrive at a chosen position. You must, then, seek to be an active contributing citizen of His realm, with God as your King. You must abdicate your throne as king of your life and seek to live according to His will for you (see Letter 1). You must stay in constant communication with Him, daily learning who this King is, and accept with gratitude your place and job in His Kingdom. Since our goal in this life is to serve Him and do His bidding, you should understand what gifts and resources He has provided for you in order to accomplish this goal. His salvation by grace allows us to be new creations filled with His Holy Spirit and to work in the Kingdom of God for as long as we live or until He returns. You are not in control; the loving, powerful, sovereign God of all creation is in control. Such a fully embraced perspective will allow you not to be anxious; you will not have to worry; and you will have no fear.

This perspective is only acquired through a progressive journey. It must start by understanding this critical concept and making that essential initial choice to seek His kingdom. His Spirit will nurture you along the way; He will teach, direct and protect you as you journey in this hostile and fearful world.

How amazing and refreshing it is to realize that we can live without worry, anxiety or fear. What a blessing. Do not wait to act upon this.

I Love You,
David

Questions

Obviously in normal life one does not have the advantage to be able to evaluate and direct their life choices with the knowledge of their future. However, the author has in these letters created such a context to press each of us to focus on specific "life issues" proactively and intentionally in our younger years so that we, as we go forward, can direct our lives toward the best of all outcomes. These general questions should be regarded as a guide for the reader, individually or as a part of a small group, to address the issue at hand and make appropriate life decisions and choices.

What is the specific "life issue" the author is concerned about in this letter?

Why does the author feel this is an important issue to bring to a person's attention in their younger years; do you agree?

How did the author seem to deal with it as a younger man? Was his means of addressing the issue done properly or improperly, consciously or subconsciously, constructively or destructively, God honoring or man honoring?

How is the author, now as an older man, recommending that the specific issue be thought about and actively addressed?

The goal of each letter is not to convince the reader to deal with the issue as the author had, but to embrace the issue and determine for themselves how they choose to regard and deal with it in their lives.

Do you agree with the author's analyses and recommended manner of addressing it?

If so, explain how you will apply it in your specific life's circumstances.

If not, please elaborate on how you view the issue and how you plan to address it as you live out the rest of your life.

What wisdom would you desire your children to receive from you on this issue to better prepare and equip them to deal with it in a truthful and God-honoring manner?

Profession and Work
Letter 5

1 Peter 4:10-11
[10] Each of you should use whatever gift you have received to serve others, as faithful stewards of God's grace in its various forms. [11] If anyone speaks, they should do so as one who speaks the very words of God. If anyone serves, they should do so with the strength God provides, so that in all things God may be praised through Jesus Christ. To him be the glory and the power for ever and ever. Amen.

Acts 13:2-3
[2] While they were worshiping the Lord and fasting, the Holy Spirit said, "Set apart for me Barnabas and Saul for the work to which I have called them." [3] So after they had fasted and prayed, they placed their hands on them and sent them off.

Dear David,

You are a doctor, a Family Physician. Medicine has traditionally been a profession honored by society. As a physician you are amongst the selected few that are permitted and entitled to know the most intimate aspects of another person: their body, thoughts, emotions, life choices and relationships. Your patients assume, unless you prove differently, that you have integrity and therefore are trustworthy, honest, wise and dependable. You have opportunities to impact people, families and communities well beyond that afforded to the average person. But with opportunity comes responsibility and accountability.

Your greater identity, however, is that you are a Christian who has been called by God to this unique profession. This identity in Christ must determine and direct how you use your opportunities and to whom you are responsible and accountable. It is important and relevant to this point that you daily remember how you entered this profession. From an early age you aspired to be a doctor. As a youngster you humanly admired those you observed in the practice of medicine and wished to emulate them, but you understood very little of the supernatural forces within you that were directing you toward and preparing you for this career. In retrospect it is apparent that God was creatively and actively orchestrating the achievement of His call upon your life. Your admission into Medical School can only be explained by the miraculous work of the Lord and, in similarly amazing ways, He continued His hand of direction and provision through your subsequent residency training, early years of practice in Capron, Virginia and then your permanent place of practice in Mahomet, Illinois. Along the way you were further molded and shaped for God's purposes as you spent time as a physician in Africa and as a teacher in a Medical School. Even the courses you taught were all divinely arranged to add a further dimension toward achieving His goal of transforming you to become the physician He desired you to be. In short, there was, and is, no question that becoming a Family Physician was God's plan for you, and it was His sovereignty over all things that brought your career into full existence.

The awareness that this journey has been the result of God's choice and work is so significant that you must thank Him every day for this privilege; you must daily understand that your efforts as a physician must glorify Him and contribute to His Kingdom. Every encounter is an opportunity to, in some degree, love unconditionally, to reflect Christ in your manner and words, to perhaps pray with your patients and to encourage people toward spiritual health. As a Family Physician you have been called to deal with each person as a whole person whose body, mind, spirit and relationships are all integrated into this unique individual God has created. When appropriate, invite them to a church to worship God, or explain the way of salvation to them. Remember, though, that you must be respectful of your patient's perspective on spiritual issues and interact in these areas only if the Spirit gives you liberty to do so; you are not to cause them to be offended such that the work of the Spirit would be countered.

You are not a physician in an overtly Christian clinic and if your efforts to address spiritual needs are not received well and brought in a negative light to those in authority, you could be confronted and disciplined. In your clinic, as in all aspects of life, you are foreign and alien to this world; Christ and your active presence "in Him" will be hated and rejected by the world if given opportunity. Every day that you are able to continue to serve Him as a Christian physician is a day that He has protected you by His power and wisdom. The spiritual war is being fought all around you as you serve Him as a physician. Be sure to take time to pray each day before you even enter the door of your clinic. Recite by memory Isaiah 40:31 and hold fast to it. You can continue to serve as He has called you from the time of your youth only as you fully rely on Him – His power, discernment, wisdom and protection.

Try to finish the race well, David.

Love,
David

Author's Addendum:

Although these specific thoughts are conveyed to a young physician, the principles here are applicable to you as you also pursue your unique and individual work or profession. You are encouraged to hear as clearly as possible God's specific directive for your life's work. Then as you are doing the work He has called you to do, daily seek His wisdom, power and protection.

Questions

Obviously in normal life one does not have the advantage to be able to evaluate and direct their life choices with the knowledge of their future. However, the author has in these letters created such a context to press each of us to focus on specific "life issues" proactively and intentionally in our younger years so that we, as we go forward, can direct our lives toward the best of all outcomes. These general questions should be regarded as a guide for the reader, individually or as a part of a small group, to address the issue at hand and make appropriate life decisions and choices.

What is the specific "life issue" the author is concerned about in this letter?

Why does the author feel this is an important issue to bring to a person's attention in their younger years; do you agree?

How did the author seem to deal with it as a younger man? Was his means of addressing the issue done properly or improperly, consciously or subconsciously, constructively or destructively, God honoring or man honoring?

How is the author, now as an older man, recommending that the specific issue be thought about and actively addressed?

The goal of each letter is not to convince the reader to deal with the issue as the author had, but to embrace the issue and determine for themselves how they choose to regard and deal with it in their lives.

Do you agree with the author's analyses and recommended manner of addressing it?

If so, explain how you will apply it in your specific life's circumstances.

If not, please elaborate on how you view the issue and how you plan to address it as you live out the rest of your life.

What wisdom would you desire your children to receive from you on this issue to better prepare and equip them to deal with it in a truthful and God-honoring manner?

Work Ethic
Letter 6

Colossians 3:23-24
[23] Whatever you do, work at it with all your heart, as working for the Lord, not for human masters, [24] since you know that you will receive an inheritance from the Lord as a reward. It is the Lord Christ you are serving.

Dear David,

There were, admittedly, some shortcomings and misdirection in your childhood-adolescent nurturing and training. In another letter (letter 10), we will confront them and rejoice in how God has since spoken into these areas and brought some resolution and completion. However, there were a few areas in these formative years that your training was notably positive, powerful and have proven, for the most part, beneficial. You arrived at your adult years with a superior "work ethic;" this is characterized by your ability to give attentive and dedicated effort, to demonstrate perseverance in the face of difficulty and demand, to display self-discipline, and to embrace and seek a high standard of accomplishment and time efficiency. You learned to press yourself for the best and seek to be the best.

Obviously, this same powerful work ethic has its downside. Even now, you rarely let yourself be content in your efforts and accomplishments, you allow your productivity to define your self-worth, you find it difficult to carve out and enjoy down or leisure time and you hold those others in your life to similar high standards. (The latter area is more transmitted by modelling and implicit teaching than by overt instruction.) Thankfully, as the Spirit has been transforming your inner person you have been able to modulate and temper these problematic aspects; however, it will take a life-time to balance this work-ethic issue.

But we should not let the negative aspects of this quality overshadow its wonderful positive aspects. The Scripture makes it clear that Jesus expects His servants to use their education, personal character traits, talents, opportunities, position, possessions and His Spirit given "gifts" to build His Kingdom: to bring people to salvation and make disciples of all who would hear and follow Him. Paul uses himself as an example of how those who serve God must persevere despite obstacles, suffering and persecution (2 Corinthians 11:16-28); he exhorts his newly founded churches to emulate him, as he emulates Christ (1 Corinthians 11:1). Although he begs God to remove the thorn in his side (2 Corinthians 12:7-10) he accepts that God chooses not to do so, and that he must in humility and dependence do his work relying upon God for strength. This is a critical point. Even though one has learned and implements a strong work ethic, it must be under the supervision of Christ so that it results in the growth of God's Kingdom and not of our self-exultating kingdom. Jesus' parable of the servants (Matthew 25:14-30) strongly teaches that we will be accountable to how we use what we have been given. Those who fruitfully use the opportunities and resources God has given them will then be expected to do even more as God further equips and opens doors of further opportunity. To be lazy and unproductive in the use of your position, abilities and gifts will bring negative judgment; while the conscientious use of them for God will yield additional rewards at judgment.

Further, Paul, Peter and James (Romans 5:3-5; 1 Peter 1:6-7; James 1:2-4) all teach with authority the benefits of hard work and perseverance in the face of persecution, suffering and difficulties. Intentionally seeking to serve Christ in this oppressive and "suffering-producing world" will require discipline, perseverance and resilience; this will produce godly character and maturity (in human and spiritual terms). Most of us can testify that hard work, even in difficult situations, yields qualitatively different and uniquely valuable lessons that equip us to serve more effectively our families, our fellow man and, of course, God.

I have found God is very creative in how He chooses to employ or implement a strong work ethic and our willingness to be available to Him. He is continually grooming and preparing us for His service; He will confront us with challenges and open up opportunities for us that we would never expect or predict. Such challenges and opportunities will not only be a way to "raise the bar" a bit further in your level of serving but will also bring you joy and an excitement to living that the world cannot provide.

Therefore, David, do not bemoan that you have learned and possess a strong work ethic, but seek to corral it and dedicate it to the adventure of living fruitfully for God.

Love,
David

Questions

Obviously in normal life one does not have the advantage to be able to evaluate and direct their life choices with the knowledge of their future. However, the author has in these letters created such a context to press each of us to focus on specific "life issues" proactively and intentionally in our younger years so that we, as we go forward, can direct our lives toward the best of all outcomes. These general questions should be regarded as a guide for the reader, individually or as a part of a small group, to address the issue at hand and make appropriate life decisions and choices.

What is the specific "life issue" the author is concerned about in this letter?

Why does the author feel this is an important issue to bring to a person's attention in their younger years; do you agree?

How did the author seem to deal with it as a younger man? Was his means of addressing the issue done properly or improperly, consciously or subconsciously, constructively or destructively, God honoring or man honoring?

How is the author, now as an older man, recommending that the specific issue be thought about and actively addressed?

The goal of each letter is not to convince the reader to deal with the issue as the author had, but to embrace the issue and determine for themselves how they choose to regard and deal with it in their lives.

Do you agree with the author's analyses and recommended manner of addressing it?

If so, explain how you will apply it in your specific life's circumstances.

If not, please elaborate on how you view the issue and how you plan to address it as you live out the rest of your life.

What wisdom would you desire your children to receive from you on this issue to better prepare and equip them to deal with it in a truthful and God-honoring manner?

From Whom Do You Seek Praise?

Letter 7

John 12:42-43
⁴² Yet at the same time many even among the leaders believed in him. But because of the Pharisees they would not openly acknowledge their faith for fear they would be put out of the synagogue. ⁴³ for they loved human praise more than praise from God.

1 Corinthians 4:5
⁵ Therefore judge nothing before the appointed time; wait until the Lord comes. He will bring to light what is hidden in darkness and will expose the motives of the heart. At that time each will receive their praise from God.

Dear David,

In this letter I would like to address another basic question that deserves your continued contemplation. It is a question that should challenge your method of making decisions and establishing priorities; it can be a useful guide in making the correct choices for yourself, your family and for serving God in the Kingdom. It is a simple question and one that is derived from Scripture. From whom, David, do you seek praise: man, or God? It, when applied, strips away the false and self-seeking motives that the world expects and endorses and directs you toward the true, important and lasting features of life (as God designed it) that you should pursue.

We are taught and modeled, from the beginning of our childhood and all through our years going forward, that the approval and recognition by other people are the evaluation standards that are to be used in life. In our profession or our work, especially, but also in our hobbies and recreation we seek to be the best, the highest and the most. We (if we are able to understand and be honest) want others, especially those who are likewise engaged in a given area, to affirm us and recognize us. The more plaques of recognition, gold stars of performance and financial bonuses that highlight our exceptional productivity, the more exalted we feel. Yet, such affirmations only satisfy in a fleeting and incomplete manner. It seems that no matter how much we are recognized by man it is not enough. We are pressed to work harder and achieve more in an effort to know that allusive soulful fulfillment. This is a race that can never be won, a goal that will never be achieved and will result in a life of deception and regret. I have talked with many people (in my work as a physician) at the end of their lives and rarely do they point to human achievement or praise of man as that which gives them deep peace and joy. Too often they deeply regret buying into the world's ways and indicate they would "do it differently if they had to do it all over." Sadly, many of these people, though, do not understand nor can they explain just how they would approach life differently in order to achieve satisfaction, peace, joy and a sense of completion. The truth that they missed was that only through a spiritual reorientation of this question could their lives have ended differently.

Jesus admonishes us to seek the praise of God, not of man; He said of the hypocritical Pharisees: ".... for they loved praise from men more than praise from God" (John 12:43). This, as in many of the issues I write to you about, requires a paradigm shift from the wisdom of this human world to the wisdom of God (1 Corinthians 2:6-16). We must seek to know God and His character, who we are in Him (our new identity) and His will for us (in all things). We then must know and appropriate the Holy Spirit, the "Spirit of Truth" that Jesus sent after His ascension (John 15:26). This Holy Spirit progressively transforms us so that we are able to accomplish that which is now becoming important and determinant: doing what God would have us do, daily and in all circumstances. In this we can experience that deep blessedness only to be found as we are approved by and have fellowship with our true father and creator; we seek to hear with spiritual ears His praise: "Well done, good and faithful servant" (Luke 19:17). This alone brings true peace, joy and a sense of completion. A life lived to please God and secure His praise will allow us, at our death, to be able to have no regrets.

Be advised, David, that you will be unable by your human strength to turn from seeking the praise of man to seeking the praise of God. The world will battle you on this and if you rely only on your human ability you will succumb to their standard; you will not succeed armed only with human resolve. It can only be accomplished and sustained by a life transformed and empowered (progressively) by the Spirit of God.

This is not only profitable for you personally but also for your daughters as you give proper direction to them as they move forward in their lives.

Love,
David

Questions

Obviously in normal life one does not have the advantage to be able to evaluate and direct their life choices with the knowledge of their future. However, the author has in these letters created such a context to press each of us to focus on specific "life issues" proactively and intentionally in our younger years so that we, as we go forward, can direct our lives toward the best of all outcomes. These general questions should be regarded as a guide for the reader, individually or as a part of a small group, to address the issue at hand and make appropriate life decisions and choices.

What is the specific "life issue" the author is concerned about in this letter?

Why does the author feel this is an important issue to bring to a person's attention in their younger years; do you agree?

How did the author seem to deal with it as a younger man? Was his means of addressing the issue done properly or improperly, consciously or subconsciously, constructively or destructively, God honoring or man honoring?

How is the author, now as an older man, recommending that the specific issue be thought about and actively addressed?

The goal of each letter is not to convince the reader to deal with the issue as the author had, but to embrace the issue and determine for themselves how they choose to regard and deal with it in their lives.

Do you agree with the author's analyses and recommended manner of addressing it?

If so, explain how you will apply it in your specific life's circumstances.

If not, please elaborate on how you view the issue and how you plan to address it as you live out the rest of your life.

What wisdom would you desire your children to receive from you on this issue to better prepare and equip them to deal with it in a truthful and God-honoring manner?

Four Challenges that Changed
My Life

Letter 8

James 1:2-4
² Consider it pure joy, my brothers and sisters, whenever you face trials of many kinds, ³ because you know that the testing of your faith produces perseverance. ⁴ Let perseverance finish its work so that you may be mature and complete, not lacking anything.

Dear David,

As we walk this journey of life, we will encounter words spoken by others that deeply sting and act to shake our fragile ego foundations. We try to lessen this pain by denying that there is truth in those words or explain them away by negatively criticizing the person who spoke them. Yet they seem to somehow manage to sear our heart and mind and, without our permission, change us. They can, however, be a cause of significant and positive personal growth despite the emotional pain they may stir up. I recall four such verbal challenges in my life that, as I look back, have impacted me and helped me to become a better person. Yet they hurt deeply when I first received them.

The first of these verbal assaults came from my own father, not once but on several occasions. I believe he loved me and felt in his heart that this challenge would motivate and help me in my development. Yet to a young man, the inner agony of those words was difficult to rise above. "David, unless you apply yourself better you will never amount to much!" These were his words; they were engraved into my soul. Through this seemingly negative judgment of my life at the point of these utterances, he was trying to encourage me toward discipline and hard work. He experienced the deprivation of life growing up in the depression years yet, by resolve and hard work, my father became the first person of his family to go to college. He felt passionately that his sons must follow this same path if they were to succeed in life. I never knew, and still don't know even as I write this letter, what he observed in me for him to conclude that I was not working hard enough. It was, though, as I reflect back, a "chancy" statement. I could, rather than improve my effort to work harder, accept this negative analysis as truth and then choose to live forever as a disappointment and a failure: "to never amount to much." Yet God became a part of my life around that time and His unconditional love and acceptance allowed me to accept my father's challenge. I developed a strong life of discipline and chose to work hard toward achieving God's goals for me in my life. (See Letter 6). I can now confront his words without feeling their sting and judgment; I can look forward with confidence that I "will finish the race well." God alone took his words and used them for His Kingdom's glory. What could possibly have brought ill to my life was used for good.

The second phrase that was formative in my life, but painful to hear at the time, came from my Pastor who was also my friend. Like my father he said these words, I am certain, believing that I needed to confront the concerns embodied in them for my betterment.

"David, you never finish what you start out to accomplish." He expanded on this indictment: "You begin well, with enthusiasm and good intentions, but lose focus and drive. You have a pattern of beginning something of value but then when confronted with obstacles, rejection, 'push-back' or questioning, you seem to disengage and give up. The project fails and the goals once embraced are never accomplished. This will weaken your usefulness in God's Kingdom." He was right, but my humanness ignited with anguish and self-condemnation. To bring glory to God in my work and to impact those I would have influence upon would require perseverance and an ability to proceed ahead toward a goal even in the face of opposition or persecution. Romans 8:17 is clear: if we are to be His disciples and enjoy His glory, we have to participate in His suffering. I needed to learn to persevere, especially if the task is directed by the will of God, despite any worldly efforts to discourage. This lesson has served me well and I have reminded myself of its truth over the years as I have tried to live for Him in the kingdom of this world.

The third accusation that severely attacked my self-valuation and confidence was perhaps the most painful. It was a written comment from an unknown medical colleague that was passed on to me by the administration of our group medical practice. "Dr. Webb is the most prideful and self-centered person I know." This cut into my soul with such force that I was left staggering for weeks. Not only was it emotionally painful but it confused me because I had never viewed myself this way and wondered what I might have said or done to evoke this opinion. I tried to dismiss it and blame it on this person's short sightedness or misunderstanding of me and my motives. I wanted to believe it to be a false view, yet it haunted me relentlessly. What if it was, at least in part, true?! This inner agony brought me in prayer to God and asked Him to allow me to confront any truth therein. I came to see that, although my true view of myself was not prideful and I did not seek intentionally to elevate myself at another's expense, my personal demeaner may, as a result of my need to achieve perfection, project to others pride and self-seeking. I needed to examine my interaction styles with others and be vigilant to try to extinguish any words and non-verbal behavior that could be interpreted as pride. I sought to better understand the concept of humility through the counsel of the Word of God. The Book of Proverbs was a solid and helpful source for my efforts to transform this human and flesh influenced trait. Even now I find that others can interpret my discipline, hard work and perseverance as self-glorifying and controlling. I find this to be a hard balance but diligently seek to not let such a perception undermine my sincere wish and goal: to glorify and serve God.

The fourth and last challenge that has impacted my life's journey was spoken by my "Advanced Biology" teacher when I was a Junior in High School. There were four of us boys, friends and academic competitors, in his class; we all aspired to become doctors. One day he took us aside and said to us: "You all want to be doctors but only one of the four of you will make it: I wonder who it shall be." This challenged me deeply and engendered, at first, fear; I was faced with a decision: give up since the odds were against success or believe in myself and set a course of hard work and perseverance. I did the latter. Yes, I was the only one of the four that became a physician; his dire prediction was correct. Yet looking back now I know that God's will and prayers – mine and others, were the determining factors. My road to become a doctor can only be explained by His intervention (See Letter 5). Although hard work, determination and diligence were and are required for goal achievement, this is not sufficient for those who seek to be His servant. Your individual goals must be consistent with God's will so that His powerful and creative presence directs and facilitates the journey (See Letter 1).

The personal qualities of discipline, hard work, perseverance and humility are to be sought after and developed by those who seek to be Christ's disciple in this world. To learn these traits and incorporate them consistently in a life requires at times a painful confrontation of our inadequacies. Although I felt the deep searing pain in my soul of these four unsolicited challenges, I am forever grateful that God brought them to my attention.

David, continue, even in your latter years, to fully live your life with these qualities. Your goal, ultimately, is to hear the Lord say: "Well done my good and faithful servant."

Love,
David

Questions

Obviously in normal life one does not have the advantage to be able to evaluate and direct their life choices with the knowledge of their future. However, the author has in these letters created such a context to press each of us to focus on specific "life issues" proactively and intentionally in our younger years so that we, as we go forward, can direct our lives toward the best of all outcomes. These general questions should be regarded as a guide for the reader, individually or as a part of a small group, to address the issue at hand and make appropriate life decisions and choices.

What is the specific "life issue" the author is concerned about in this letter?

Why does the author feel this is an important issue to bring to a person's attention in their younger years; do you agree?

How did the author seem to deal with it as a younger man? Was his means of addressing the issue done properly or improperly, consciously or subconsciously, constructively or destructively, God honoring or man honoring?

How is the author, now as an older man, recommending that the specific issue be thought about and actively addressed?

The goal of each letter is not to convince the reader to deal with the issue as the author had, but to embrace the issue and determine for themselves how they choose to regard and deal with it in their lives.

Do you agree with the author's analyses and recommended manner of addressing it?

If so, explain how you will apply it in your specific life's circumstances.

If not, please elaborate on how you view the issue and how you plan to address it as you live out the rest of your life.

What wisdom would you desire your children to receive from you on this issue to better prepare and equip them to deal with it in a truthful and God-honoring manner?

A Life Well Lived
Letter 9

Acts 11:22-24
²² News of this reached the church in Jerusalem, and they sent Barnabas to Antioch. ²³ When he arrived and saw what the grace of God had done, he was glad and encouraged them all to remain true to the Lord with all their hearts. ²⁴ He was a good man, full of the Holy Spirit and faith, and a great number of people were brought to the Lord.

1 John 4:19-21
¹⁹ We love because he first loved us. ²⁰ Whoever claims to love God yet hates a brother or sister is a liar. For whoever does not love their brother and sister, whom they have seen, cannot love God, whom they have not seen. ²¹ And he has given us this command: Anyone who loves God must also love their brother and sister.

Dear David,

You are prone to "pondering" – the work of reflecting deeply upon some concept, observation or truth. The purpose and benefit of such "work" is to try to understand God more and apply this understanding to how one lives their life more fully and effectively. Through pondering and the resolve it can bring forth, one is able to better direct their life purposefully. Pondering begins with asking yourself a question, often a complex one whose answer is not readily apparent. In this letter I want to focus upon one such question – one that I have been wrestling with for many years. The question is: "How do you measure the value of a life well lived?"

This question begs inquiry upon three word concepts embodied within it. To understand and be enriched by this question requires one to maul over each of these concepts, and then draw an overall conclusion. Such a conclusion would, or should, compel you to live differently and with more clarity of purpose. Be aware, however, that most people find this challenge intimidating, overwhelming or fearful; they decline (usually without seriously confronting the question) to complicate or "dramatize" their life in this way. I write to urging you to confront this question, ponder it and allow it to speak into you deep and life altering wisdom.

Firstly, you must ask what characterizes a "life well lived?" The world has many answers for this and will indeed answer it for you if you do not choose an answer for yourself. The world's answers generally revolve around the acquisition of power, wealth and position. According to this view, the more money you can accumulate, the more material things you will possess and the more power you can hold in society, the better you have lived your life. With this view you would seek to control your life in order to maximize your wealth and power. "Success" (a worldly term for "a life well lived?") is thus so defined and enculturated. It is evident by this definition that worldly success flows naturally out of the basic human sins of pride and self-exaltation. But, David, is this truth? Can this "success" be what God had intended for us as a life well lived? The answer is indeed "No;" a life well lived is a God controlled life that has as its purpose to glorify and serve Him. In this we find completion and fulfillment, peace and joy. This state of being is encapsulated and summarized in the Jewish concept of shalom. Shalom is the state where everything in creation is as God intended it to be. A life well lived must reject the world's way and seek true shalom.

A life well lived begins with establishing and growing your relationship with your creator. Unless you seek to conform to that which you were designed ("hard wired") to be, you will never in your soul know this shalom. Once this relationship has been established (through Christ's work on the cross), God provides the Holy Spirit to indwell and transform a person. John 16 explains that the Spirit enables us to truly know our fallen human condition and how we are to transcend it: The Spirit guides us into truth and proper understanding; He allows us to know the mind of God. In short, God's powerful transforming work in one's life redefines what "a life well lived" should look like. Only as we can see life through God's eyes and align our will with His can we hope to accurately answer that question and live it out. Each person's life will be unique and personalized (by the Spirits molding) but will hold in common the goal of living as God created each of us to live. Therefore "a life well lived" is a beautiful and dynamic enactment of the vertical relationship with our creator.

The second concept imbedded in this question is that of "value." A life well lived must bring something valuable out of our existence. If a life lived does not result in an identifiable value, then it is not being well lived – your life has missed its mark! Value is a concept that is generally not critically thought about by a person and by default has been subtly and covertly defined by the world in terms of self: "My life is valuable if I am happy and have what I want."

But true value is not measurable by self-parameters but by the impact a life, well lived, makes upon other people or God's Kingdom. Have we impacted positively the life of at least one person; have we contributed positively to a group of people or a segment of society that is in need; have we added to or championed a godly cause; have we stood against evil in the world and promoted God's moral standard? To live a life that brings such value requires sacrifice, a choice that benefits others rather than seeking one's own selfish desires. Value achievement in life is the outworking of sacrificial, selfless love. Understanding this concept of value brings us face-to-face with the reality that this cannot be accomplished in our human wisdom and strength. We, in our natural state, are not able to love unconditionally and sacrificially. Value achievement for and in this world is accomplishable only as we are transformed by the Spirit and live in Christ. What is good, true, right and proper is able to be known, chosen by us and diligently employed only out of such a relationship.

Thirdly, the question asks how are we to "measure" this value enacted by a life well lived? The answer to this inquiry is closely connected with the "value issue" just discussed and can be understood as the quantitative arm of this concept. To measure something requires some means to quantitate and make an assessment. How do we quantitate our efforts to live valuably – to perpetrate that which is good, true, right and proper? I have come to believe that the only true measure is the influence, effect and impact we can have on another person. Has another person experienced true sacrificial love from us so that they have been changed, redirected or given new vitality to their existence in this world? Have we been used by God as an instrument of light and life for others? What will be your legacy as you exit this human life; how will you be remembered? It is the testimony of others as to how you lived a life of value that will be the "yard stick" to assess your years on earth. The things of this world (i.e. "success") will not have any lasting value to others or to God's Kingdom. Only how you sought to know and love another will be remembered, because you have altered the very fabric of that other's life. We certainly don't "count" or keep a list of those we impact during our life; we don't focus on our human effort. Instead we walk daily alert to, sensitive to, and willing to obey the leading of the Spirit to reach out and connect with others. We will be "measured" by how well we reflected Christ and served God as His instruments for bringing to others the life He intends for them.

In summary, David, a life well lived is to be understood through a spiritual and relational definition; our value is understood by how well we bring God's intended life to this broken world, and this is measured in terms of changed lives. This perspective, as you progressively embrace and employ it, will become the heart of your being and direct every aspect of your life. In the end you can truly hear and know the blessing of God's soft and powerful voice saying: "Well done, my good and faithful servant."

Love,
David

Questions

Obviously in normal life one does not have the advantage to be able to evaluate and direct their life choices with the knowledge of their future. However, the author has in these letters created such a context to press each of us to focus on specific "life issues" proactively and intentionally in our younger years so that we, as we go forward, can direct our lives toward the best of all outcomes. These general questions should be regarded as a guide for the reader, individually or as a part of a small group, to address the issue at hand and make appropriate life decisions and choices.

What is the specific "life issue" the author is concerned about in this letter?

Why does the author feel this is an important issue to bring to a person's attention in their younger years; do you agree?

How did the author seem to deal with it as a younger man? Was his means of addressing the issue done properly or improperly, consciously or subconsciously, constructively or destructively, God honoring or man honoring?

How is the author, now as an older man, recommending that the specific issue be thought about and actively addressed?

The goal of each letter is not to convince the reader to deal with the issue as the author had, but to embrace the issue and determine for themselves how they choose to regard and deal with it in their lives.

Do you agree with the author's analyses and recommended manner of addressing it?

If so, explain how you will apply it in your specific life's circumstances.

If not, please elaborate on how you view the issue and how you plan to address it as you live out the rest of your life.

What wisdom would you desire your children to receive from you on this issue to better prepare and equip them to deal with it in a truthful and God-honoring manner?

Part 2
Marriage and Family

Family of Origin
Letter 10

2 Corinthians 5:16-21
¹⁶ So from now on we regard no one from a worldly point of view. Though we once regarded Christ in this way, we do so no longer. ¹⁷ Therefore, if anyone is in Christ, the new creation has come: The old has gone, the new is here! ¹⁸ All this is from God, who reconciled us to himself through Christ and gave us the ministry of reconciliation: ¹⁹ that God was reconciling the world to himself in Christ, not counting people's sins against them. And he has committed to us the message of reconciliation. ²⁰ We are therefore Christ's ambassadors, as though God were making his appeal through us. We implore you on Christ's behalf: Be reconciled to God. ²¹ God made him who had no sin to be sin for us, so that in him we might become the righteousness of God.

1 Timothy 5:8
⁸ Anyone who does not provide for their relatives, and especially for their own household, has denied the faith and is worse than an unbeliever.

Dear David,

It is human to want to distance oneself from that which brings distress: rejection, insecurity and fear, or from that which seeks to expose painful memories. Although your years in your family of origin established some personal traits that resulted in you accomplishing much positively in life (such as a high work ethic, a striving for excellence and a sensitive heart), there were some deep and dark experiences and occurrences that have negatively impacted you and your life. These have stained and seared you enough that, without intentionally choosing so, you distanced yourself from your parents and brothers. Your relationship with Judy (begun early in your older adolescent years) was deeply positive, satisfying and exciting. As that relationship progressed you found it easy to move away from the original family and toward establishing your own new and comfortable family. The demands of your medical education and training legitimized your "inability" to live geographically close to them or be available to visit them or be a part of their lives. When you then moved your newly formed family to the Midwest you continued to have a practical and reasonable excuse for maintaining a distant relationship. Most significantly, however, to this separation was the reality that as your faith grew you felt increasingly alien or as a stranger to this family of origin since they did not share your emerging spiritual identity. As you began raising your daughters the demands of young children only added to this distancing. Although somewhat deceptive but understandable, you offered as a reason for your non-involvement a lack of time and a demanding schedule (yours and the kids'). Therefore, for many years your new nuclear family was geographically and relationally separated and distant from your parents and your brothers (now out of the house and building their own families as well). When your Mom and Dad divorced, and through the hurtful years preceding that, you felt further legitimized to retreat from them; you did not want to expose your young daughter to this "mayhem." They, after all, had "proper grandparents" to relate to in Judy's parents; her parents were present and important in the life of your young family.

Once this reality was established, expectations adjusted and you had found ways to dismiss any sense of guilt or extended family responsibility, it was easy to minimize all forms of communication. Phone calls, cards, or letters became scarce and superficial. Often when your nuclear family celebrated events or milestones in Champaign – Mahomet, you didn't even think to extend an invitation to your parents or brothers.

The result was that, on the positive side, you and your nuclear family could have the freedom to establish your own composite identity with its foundation in Christ. The relational strain and the toxic effect of words and actions that characterized too often the previous years could no longer cause harm to you, your marriage or your children. The negative environment of the past no longer had opportunity to influence the choices you had to make as your family grew and developed. There was a sense of emotional relief and a longed-for peace. The climate felt hospitable and warm; a better place for people to become all that God desired for them. This separation also, as it turned out, gave you time for reflection, to seek to gain understanding and begin you on a road toward forgiveness and reconciliation.

Yet, as I now reflect back, it was, in part, a selfish and unloving response. I grieve that my parents and brothers were functionally not a part of our lives – especially the lives of our daughters. My mother had so much love she wished to give and a deep desire to be a grandmother, although her good intentions were often insensitively and inappropriately directed. For her to have more opportunity to be a part of our family would have brought her great joy and comfort. She died unhappy and unfulfilled. (I must clarify however, only in a small degree was her unhappiness due to my choices.) My father chose a life that reflected his self-centeredness and emotional selfishness. But I wonder if I should have sought God's direction as how to best honor him and extract his "hidden wisdom," a wisdom that could have been helpful in my later adult years. Progressively I have come to view him with pity because I do believe he deeply cared for his sons but didn't know how to express it in a helpful and affirming manner.

Your brothers defined their own journeys as they also dealt with the realities of your family of origin. They chose individually unique paths that were divergent enough from yours that relationships with them also grew cold and at times subtly conflictual. Yet in retrospect I see they were also deeply hurting and if we could have grown in closeness we could have supported, nurtured and helped one another. Even if our spiritual perspectives were different, I think there would be enough common ground that unified us so that we could have better flourished as individuals and as families. I also wonder that if we could have been able to remain connected (to an effective functional degree) I could have better served Christ as a testimony to Him and His ethic for living. I had found true life and the "light" that can shine through the darkness and gloom of the flesh, but I had no legitimate and sanctioned relationship with my brothers to offer them the truth I had found. Except for one brother, their lives had been so directed away from Christianity that they may still have rejected it and me, but at least the seeds of the faith would have been planted. Perhaps in the context of a caring relationship these faith seeds might not have been so immediately rejected. As a result of my choice to detach from them, my faith witness was negatively regarded as they viewed me with some legitimate anger and resentment.

As I now reflect back, I see that even in this complex and fractured family situation, God was powerful enough to indwell even those meager and awkward interactions I was able to have with my parents. Miraculously both my mother and father accepted Christ before their deaths. I continue to pray for and seek to be a witness to my brothers but even at this writing two of them continue to reject Christ and distance themselves from this part of my identity.

In recent years God has showed me that I need to reconcile and slowly rebuild proper relationships with my brothers. I do not feel a great guilt or remorse over the path I chose since it was, I believe, a necessary path to allow my marriage and relationships with my daughters to be what God would have them to be. This journey was also necessary to bring me to the point that I can honestly love my brothers and accept them where they are. I needed to heal and forgive; I needed to mature enough to see things less selfishly, all made possible through the process of a spiritual transformation.

As you, David, move forward in your life, please finish as quickly as possible the emotional, relational and spiritual work you need to do so that you can love your family of origin. Of course, do not jeopardize the welfare and culture of your home, but seek to understand the past with fresh intentions and a positive attitude. Then sacrificially make proactive steps to grow closer to your parents and brothers. It is right; it will bring glory to God and blessing to you and the kids. At your age it is not too late to honor your parents and halt the progressive estrangement that will take place with your brothers. Time is precious and a commodity that once lost cannot be recovered; use your time now wisely and powerfully. Make this a subject of your prayer life and an area of wrestling with God. He can overcome all obstacles and will do amazing things for you in this area of your family's life.

Love,
David

Questions

Obviously in normal life one does not have the advantage to be able to evaluate and direct their life choices with the knowledge of their future. However, the author has in these letters created such a context to press each of us to focus on specific "life issues" proactively and intentionally in our younger years so that we, as we go forward, can direct our lives toward the best of all outcomes. These general questions should be regarded as a guide for the reader, individually or as a part of a small group, to address the issue at hand and make appropriate life decisions and choices.

What is the specific "life issue" the author is concerned about in this letter?

Why does the author feel this is an important issue to bring to a person's attention in their younger years; do you agree?

How did the author seem to deal with it as a younger man? Was his means of addressing the issue done properly or improperly, consciously or subconsciously, constructively or destructively, God honoring or man honoring?

How is the author, now as an older man, recommending that the specific issue be thought about and actively addressed?

The goal of each letter is not to convince the reader to deal with the issue as the author had, but to embrace the issue and determine for themselves how they choose to regard and deal with it in their lives.

Do you agree with the author's analyses and recommended manner of addressing it?

If so, explain how you will apply it in your specific life's circumstances.

If not, please elaborate on how you view the issue and how you plan to address it as you live out the rest of your life.

What wisdom would you desire your children to receive from you on this issue to better prepare and equip them to deal with it in a truthful and God-honoring manner?

Choosing Your Spouse

Letter 11

2 Corinthians 6:14-15
14 Do not be yoked together with unbelievers. For what do righteousness and wickedness have in common? Or what fellowship can light have with darkness? 15 What harmony is there between Christ and Belial? Or what does a believer have in common with an unbeliever?

Ephesians 5:21, 31-33
21 Submit to one another out of reverence for Christ.

31 "For this reason a man will leave his father and mother and be united to his wife, and the two will become one flesh." 32 This is a profound mystery—but I am talking about Christ and the church. 33 However, each one of you also must love his wife as he loves himself, and the wife must respect her husband.

Dear David,

I debated a while about whether it is profitable for me to write you concerning this topic: the importance of choosing the proper mate. My quandary was not that this issue is of questionable importance (for I believe it is the second most critically important decision a person makes) but its relevance to you in your current stage of life. You have already chosen a wife. But you will have an opportunity and responsibility to direct and counsel those who have not yet made their choice, especially your daughters. Therefore, here are my thoughts and reflections.

In this area, like most of life's decisions, we find ourselves engaged in a battle with what is right, good and beneficial from God's perspective as opposed to what the world defines and powerfully directs. God has a definite will, in all matters of our life, that reflects His sovereign wisdom, but if we do not seek to know and follow this then we are at the mercy of the values, priorities, passions and time-pressures of our particular society and generational standards. We are flooded daily by words, pictures and examples of what the world offers as the "desirable" (not necessarily correct) spouse: one that would satisfy our human passions and physical needs. These passions and needs pound within us (especially in our teenage and younger adult years) seeking outlets for expression. The combination of the world's messages and our flesh needs make us vulnerable to temptations and will, if God doesn't intervene, cause us to succumb to making the wrong and destructive choice for a mate in marriage.

Before going any further, it is worthwhile to ponder the question: "Why is it so important (critical) to choose properly concerning a spouse?" As I consider scripture, I believe God created every individual as incomplete as a single person and only in an intimate union with another of the opposite gender can we hope to be complete and adequate to have fellowship with and serve God in our world. I should add a disclaimer here: I do believe that there are those who are to live as single people and able to serve God dynamically, but these are the exceptions and must be God selected and God empowered to do so. In Genesis God provided a "help-mate" to Adam; he and Eve were "to become one flesh:" a new and better being. The intent and plan of God was that only as we are unified (a man and a woman) are we "one;" there is a beautiful, intricate and wise collective "being" that is formed in the marital union. Each person supplements, encourages, strengthens, contributes, satisfies and increases the other. The need for relational intimacy (at all levels) is God created and reflects the intimacy within the Godhead. His deep desire was for us, His creation, to have that same relational intimacy with Him as our creator. In His wisdom, He determine that this can best be accomplished as each person relates to Him in the context of that unique union called marriage. Additionally, children can best be properly nurtured and prepared to live proper godly lives in the context of a family formed upon the foundation of marriage. Yet I do acknowledge, as an exception to this, that single people can raise such children but here again only by God's choice and empowerment.

Our service to God in His Kingdom can be fulfilled best, to the extent He intended, if each person is secure and enabled by being "one" with a (God-chosen) spouse, and that couple in turn becomes integrally a part of the expanded "body of Christ" – the local church (The issue of church will be addressed in letter 21). Service in His Kingdom may be by each individual within the marriage acting independently or by the unified couple acting as one flesh. In my experience (and I believe by God's intent) the proper God serving marriage should foster both: each individual pursuing their unique ministry as well as the unified couple engaging together in the work of the Kingdom.

I strongly believe that physical – sexual intimacy is good, and God ordained; we are to mutually enjoy our created bodies and through this intimacy we are energized to persevere in our service in His Kingdom here on earth. Yet the full and effective benefit and blessing of sexual intimacy can only find its expression in the context of a lifelong commitment of one person to another; a commitment where sacrificial love places a spouse's needs above our own. Thus, even in the area of physical intimacy one person seeks to unselfishly fulfill their spouse; their own pleasure dependent upon the personal satisfaction of the one they love sacrificially.

This "right spouse" is chosen, not by human ability but by God's wisdom and will. Human criteria, as I have said, will most likely lead to a wrong choice, an unfulfilled life and a great deal of pain and suffering. Every young person must firstly desire to know God's choice for them, then secondly make it a daily prayer concern. Thirdly, they are to seek from older and more spiritually mature people (hopefully including parents) their experiential wisdom and their understanding of Biblical truth concerning this subject. Fourthly, they are to discipline themselves to relate socially to those who hold these same objections and are also trying to resist the world's influence in this area. This, of course, will restrict the options of where and under what pretense they will allow themselves to spend time and develop relationships. Fifthly, each person must firmly commit to and participate in relationships with those of the opposite gender in ways that do not involve (other than very superficially) physical contact. The human flesh is not to be trusted when passions are ignited by too sensual a touch. It is an area of vulnerability; it is very easy to be blinded by our passions, not establish wise boundaries and rationalize succumbing to destructive temptations. Inappropriate physical intimacy will weaken the development of the proper and foundational relationship required for a lasting and fulfilling marriage. Also, it can set a tone in the relationship of compromised integrity (letter 2) and disrespect and dishonor for the other person (letter 25). In summary as you approach the subject of choosing the right spouse, you must walk this important but tenuous journey with your eyes and ears open, expecting and prepared to discern God's leadings and His choice.

I must add here yet another disclaimer: Although I believe in and recommend strongly what I have written above, God is sovereign and is in complete control of all situations. If a person deviates from these suggestions and does not really seek God's choice, he or she may still find themselves married to the best and right spouse. I suspect this could be so because others (especially parents) had been praying diligently for a specific young person. God has directed their choice even though they were not themselves seeking His direction, and despite their human and improperly determined means for seeking their future spouse. But we should not count on this or assume He will protect and direct us despite ourselves.

David, you choose well in this area, but if we are to be honest, you did not completely follow God on this journey; yet He did lead you and Judy together in marriage. His gracious gift in your wonderful marriage should forever be acknowledged with a deep sense of gratitude and thanksgiving. Do your best to direct your daughters and grandchildren in the proper seeking of God's choice for their spouse.

Love,
David

Questions

Obviously in normal life one does not have the advantage to be able to evaluate and direct their life choices with the knowledge of their future. However, the author has in these letters created such a context to press each of us to focus on specific "life issues" proactively and intentionally in our younger years so that we, as we go forward, can direct our lives toward the best of all outcomes. These general questions should be regarded as a guide for the reader, individually or as a part of a small group, to address the issue at hand and make appropriate life decisions and choices.

What is the specific "life issue" the author is concerned about in this letter?

Why does the author feel this is an important issue to bring to a person's attention in their younger years; do you agree?

How did the author seem to deal with it as a younger man? Was his means of addressing the issue done properly or improperly, consciously or subconsciously, constructively or destructively, God honoring or man honoring?

How is the author, now as an older man, recommending that the specific issue be thought about and actively addressed?

The goal of each letter is not to convince the reader to deal with the issue as the author had, but to embrace the issue and determine for themselves how they choose to regard and deal with it in their lives.

Do you agree with the author's analyses and recommended manner of addressing it?

If so, explain how you will apply it in your specific life's circumstances.

If not, please elaborate on how you view the issue and how you plan to address it as you live out the rest of your life.

What wisdom would you desire your children to receive from you on this issue to better prepare and equip them to deal with it in a truthful and God-honoring manner?

Adult Friends
Letter 12

John 11:28-36
²⁸ After she had said this, she went back and called her sister Mary aside. "The Teacher is here," she said, "and is asking for you." ²⁹ When Mary heard this, she got up quickly and went to him. ³⁰ Now Jesus had not yet entered the village but was still at the place where Martha had met him. ³¹ When the Jews who had been with Mary in the house, comforting her, noticed how quickly she got up and went out, they followed her, supposing she was going to the tomb to mourn there.
³² When Mary reached the place where Jesus was and saw him, she fell at his feet and said, "Lord, if you had been here, my brother would not have died."
³³ When Jesus saw her weeping, and the Jews who had come along with her also weeping, he was deeply moved in spirit and troubled. ³⁴ "Where have you laid him?" he asked.
"Come and see, Lord," they replied.
³⁵ Jesus wept.
³⁶ Then the Jews said, "See how he loved him!"

Proverbs 12:26, 18:24
²⁶ The righteous choose their friends carefully, but the way of the wicked leads them astray.

²⁴ One who has unreliably friends soon comes to ruin, but there is a friend who sticks closer than a brother.

Dear David,

Relationships are fundamental to being human; the ability and desire to relate to another person distinguishes us from the animal world. Since God is relational, the trinity (Father, Son and Holy Spirit) being the perfect relational community, and since we are created "in His Image," we have within our soul this need and ability. I have discussed in other letters our relationship to the Godhead, our spouse, our children and our extended family. I would like in this letter to discuss our relationship to friends.

I have observed that, with few exceptions, most older adults have very few true friends. I find this ironic since the seeking out of friends is so important and of such a high priority for older children, teens and young adults. Commonly, people, in their developmental years, look to peers outside of their family for approval and as a means to establish their value as a person; this self-worth issue is a major task for the evolving individual. Because of this, for instance, most teens have a pressing, almost desperate, need for peer approval in order to like themselves and be able to engage successfully the complexities of life.

Yet, someplace along the time-line that brings us to middle adulthood, the issue of making and maintaining friendships fades in its priority and the effort required for this is diverted elsewhere. I have also observed in adults that the time and effort committed to "having friends" varies between individuals and is influenced by their personality and how they view their worth as a person. Some personalities are more outgoing and vivacious than others and more easily, and more comfortably, enter into multiple relationships. In some cases, if the adult doesn't view themselves as valuable and secure, they will not be confident to engage in potentially demanding and time-consuming relationships. More common, it seems to me, is the situation that the necessary work of establishing our value as a person is felt to be completed sufficiently by adulthood that most adults are not driven by this agenda and need. As a result, most older adults have family relationships (at various degrees of intimacy), superficial acquaintances, task or hobby specific interactions or functional connectedness with others (need to "get a job done"). We relate to those whom we must in order to accomplish our work or life's tasks, to those who share a specific interest with us (but only interact together on <u>that</u> interest), or to a vast number of people who we know by name and exchange, from time to time, a sentence or two. Exceptionally, I do know of older adults who admirably have prioritized and made the needed effort to maintain a few true "friendships."

Although these observations may reflect reality in our modern society, I want to advocate that you make an effort to counter this movement in your life going forward. To not go the route that our culture encourages requires that you be enlightened to the issue and proactive in countering what is likely to be otherwise. As we relate more and more "electronically" (our modern age), it will be easier and easier to ignore or suppress our relational DNA and find ourselves increasingly isolated and relationally lonely. As this is happening in our human relational world, the desire and ability to relate to God in a spiritual world also becomes less and less likely. This, of course, is the goal of the enemy as he distorts our humanity and dishonors our "made in God's image" origins.

Part of the problem is that we have lost sight of what defines a "true friendship." True friendships must be built upon a foundation of "otherness;" they cannot be built upon self-seeking needs and motives, but upon a desire to know, encourage and benefit another person. Such a perspective of otherness is derived from of our identity of being "in Christ." We, to say it succinctly, must die to self if we are to have a true and intimate relationship with another person. This can only be accomplished through a spiritual transformation that changes us at our core. Our value as a person is established properly not by peer approval but as we know and receive God's love and approval. Our self-worth is found as we are "in Christ" and reside with dignity and honor in the church. Only then are we secure and confidently able to truly know the other person and be willing to let them know us deeply and honestly. When our friendships are no longer a vehicle to get our self-centered needs met or to better oneself in society, then we can allow ourselves to be real and vulnerable. When we are "other focused" we enjoy a higher degree of emotional stability and strength that will sustain a relationship through the inevitable challenges and obstacles that all relationships will encounter over time.

Friendships seem to flourish and are more sustainable if both parties share some common background or interests. Doing things together provides opportunities to be present with one another and it provides a relaxed environment for deeper sharing to occur. True friendships require an investment of time, prioritization and effort. For this reason, one cannot attempt to maintain but a few true friendships. Our lives are busy with family requirements (at multiple levels), work, church and community; to try to find the time and emotional energy to build and maintain friendships will be a limiting factor. Yet I don't think we need more than a few true friends (the number will vary relative to each person's life circumstances and their personality) to know the blessing of friendship. Therefore, seek God's direction in this area and act to build these friendships as He identifies those in whose life you should invest; do not let life's obstacles interfere with this goal.

David, to be known by (deeply and transparently) and to be able to trust and rely upon another person in any and all circumstances is a true blessing that God has intended for His human creation. To be able to call upon another to mutually enjoy an aspect of life, to talk with or share about each of your lives, to know that there is someone who will be there when you need them, to be vulnerable emotionally in their presence, to confidently realize you will be accepted and acceptable no matter what mistakes you make, and to build memories together as you encounter life over years of time, is one of the most special of God-given privileges that we have as His special creation.

I must, though, give a word of caution. Be very careful about friendships with people of the opposite gender. Remember you still have a flesh nature that can be manipulated by Satan and what may have begun as an innocent "friend-like" interaction could violate (at least emotionally) and distract you from the most important of all friendships – that with your wife. If you believe God is calling you to such a friendship, I would urge you to do so in conjunction with Judy, and possibly make this a "couple-to-couple" friendship. As a general rule, engage personal friendships only with other men and do not trust yourself in one-to-one relationship with another woman.

Lastly, I encourage you to seek at least one relationship with another who is in some or many ways different from you. This could be in the area of childhood background, life's experiences, ethnicity or race. Their interests (beyond at least one you both hold mutually) may be different than yours and their goals and aspirations in life divergent (but proper and wholesome) from yours. Such friendships broaden and enrich your life and enlarge your understanding of God. As you see life from your friends' perspectives you might be brought to focus on new aspects of this world that require attention and effort. God, I have found, often speaks deeply through friends on issues that I have ignored or resisted. We can be better equipped as a result of such friendships to make a difference in the world as we serve Him in His Spiritual Kingdom.

David, I wish that I had understood this issue of friendship better and had been more proactive to pursue and enjoy them.

Love,
David

Questions

Obviously in normal life one does not have the advantage to be able to evaluate and direct their life choices with the knowledge of their future. However, the author has in these letters created such a context to press each of us to focus on specific "life issues" proactively and intentionally in our younger years so that we, as we go forward, can direct our lives toward the best of all outcomes. These general questions should be regarded as a guide for the reader, individually or as a part of a small group, to address the issue at hand and make appropriate life decisions and choices.

What is the specific "life issue" the author is concerned about in this letter?

Why does the author feel this is an important issue to bring to a person's attention in their younger years; do you agree?

How did the author seem to deal with it as a younger man? Was his means of addressing the issue done properly or improperly, consciously or subconsciously, constructively or destructively, God honoring or man honoring?

How is the author, now as an older man, recommending that the specific issue be thought about and actively addressed?

The goal of each letter is not to convince the reader to deal with the issue as the author had, but to embrace the issue and determine for themselves how they choose to regard and deal with it in their lives.

Do you agree with the author's analyses and recommended manner of addressing it?

If so, explain how you will apply it in your specific life's circumstances.

If not, please elaborate on how you view the issue and how you plan to address it as you live out the rest of your life.

What wisdom would you desire your children to receive from you on this issue to better prepare and equip them to deal with it in a truthful and God-honoring manner?

Child Nurturing: Two Suggestions

Letter 13

Ephesians 5:15-16
15 Be very careful, then, how you live—not as unwise but as wise, 16 making the most of every opportunity, because the days are evil.

Ephesians 6:4
4 Fathers, do not exasperate your children; instead, bring them up in the training and instruction of the Lord.

Dear David,

Perhaps the most important work you must do in this life, and for the Kingdom of God, is to properly nurture your children. Ironically, even though this is true and generally agreed upon, most people are poorly trained and have not had good role models or examples to prepare them for this privilege and responsibility. You have now two young daughters and you will have more in the years to come. Then in time you will be a grandfather. You and Judy are now at the beginning of the most rewarding but also the most crucial and formative time for your children's lives.

I cannot possibly speak to all the various and multiple issues relating to child-raising and godly nurturing. However, in this letter, I would like to focus on two aspects of this process that I have found to be both effective and mutually enjoyable to me and to our children. They require minimal planning and are easily incorporated into the daily life of a family. They are useful for the individual development of the young person and powerfully positive in building a relationship between you and each of them. It takes no special skill or training but does require time and prioritization. Within each of these two areas of interaction you must be alert to and willing to capture that "teachable moment." Be prepared to allow yourself to be open and vulnerable to your child. As you have occasion to reveal your personal journey, they will better understand how godly character is formed. You must be warm and non-judgmental; you must be willing to listen to their words and their heart.

The first of these nurturing scenarios takes place when you are simply working with your child to accomplish a goal, a chore, a project, an assignment or a hobby. The specific activity that you work together on or toward is variable – it will be different for each child and change as they mature and become differentiated. You must keep your eyes and ears open to opportunities as they present themselves naturally. Be ready to take immediate advantage of them and make them a priority. Throw yourself fully into working alongside your young person but resist the urge to do it for them and don't impose upon them your adult standards. If it is their project, you are there primarily to assist and direct them. Sometimes the activity would be regarded as physical "work." If this is the case, do not simply assign them work and later return to inspect it; you should work alongside of them. The importance of this for modeling and building your child's character is not in the result of the activity but what transpires in the process of working together on it. It is time that provides a conducive environment for them to speak about and share various aspects of their life. What they speak about often is not even related to the project at hand. To your surprise they will bring up areas of their life that they are silently dealing with and that you would never had guessed or been aware of otherwise. In a casual, not emotionally charged, atmosphere kids will reveal critically important and amazing intimate aspects of their current life. The term "no big deal" is kid code: it indicates that that topic is of such emotional importance that they have to use those words to defuse it. They are uncomfortable if we, as parents, display, in our words or body language, that we are seriously affected by their revelation; they don't want us to focus too much upon it. They also do not want us to solve it for them; do not try to tell them what to do but share how you dealt with similar issues in your life and what those experiences have taught you. The sharing or questions that arise when you are in the midst of "doing" something with them usually originate out of what is at the center of that child's life at that moment. In this setting he or she feels safe, cared about and permitted to be honest and real. You can also add additional thoughts and reflections relevant to that topic throughout your time together, or when you pause for a break or a snack. They will let you know by their body language or their words when they have heard enough and need to sink back into their quiet self. This approach is especially helpful for teenagers but remember they might at any time put up their shield of protective emotions. During this process you are also teaching and demonstrating practical skills, problem solving, perseverance, priority stratification and the value of hard work. Amongst my treasured possessions are two photos: one given to me by my then 8-year-old grandson with the caption: "I love working outside with you," and another given to me by my then 6-year-old granddaughter with the caption: "I love you because you make things with me!" This way of nurturing yields powerful and unique opportunities to pour into your children and mold them into God's child.

The second area I have found satisfying and effective toward achieving your goal of raising your children to becoming strong, stable and productive adults is that time after you put them into their bed, just before the lights are turned out and they fall asleep. Because of my professional work schedule, I too often would not be home until after dinner, but I always strived to be home at the child's bedtime. It became (sort of evolved – we didn't make this an intentional decision) my parental "job" to put each child to bed. Quickly a wonderful routine emerged that allowed and encouraged a time for honest and intimate sharing. I liked to tell stories (appropriate to their age and gender), so I usually would tell first a "make-believe" story, often about animals dealing with relational or self problems – problems similar to what they (the kids) might be dealing with at that time. Then I would tell a Bible story that would relate to the same issue emphasized in the make-believe story. The stories were chosen because of some clue I had (or their mother had) of the issues that were current in their life. After the stories and before we prayed together there was, understood by me and them, time during which they could ask <u>any</u> question they wanted, or tell me <u>anything</u> that was on their mind. They knew that these things would be kept only between the two of us (and their mother) and there would never be any judgment expressed. Yes, I would guide and encourage them to seek solutions in a way that was good and beneficial (they knew the Bible was my standard) but they knew that nothing they could say would lessen my love for them. The atmosphere at their bedside was incredibly warm, secure, safe and supportive. I was often amazed at what they shared and often walked away tearful and feeling blessed and privileged to have had that time with them. Powerful and life changing seeds of wise and godly living were, I believed, planted during these moments, and a relationship of unique parent-child intimacy was enjoyed and modeled. These were teaching moments extraordinaire!

I am, David, urging you as a father to discern and consistently appropriate these two nurturing opportunities in your family's life. Seek God and His wisdom on this and allow the Holy Spirit to reveal these and other such teaching opportunities. Be intentional toward seeking how to best raise up godly children.

    Love,
    David

Questions

Obviously in normal life one does not have the advantage to be able to evaluate and direct their life choices with the knowledge of their future. However, the author has in these letters created such a context to press each of us to focus on specific "life issues" proactively and intentionally in our younger years so that we, as we go forward, can direct our lives toward the best of all outcomes. These general questions should be regarded as a guide for the reader, individually or as a part of a small group, to address the issue at hand and make appropriate life decisions and choices.

What is the specific "life issue" the author is concerned about in this letter?

Why does the author feel this is an important issue to bring to a person's attention in their younger years; do you agree?

How did the author seem to deal with it as a younger man? Was his means of addressing the issue done properly or improperly, consciously or subconsciously, constructively or destructively, God honoring or man honoring?

How is the author, now as an older man, recommending that the specific issue be thought about and actively addressed?

The goal of each letter is not to convince the reader to deal with the issue as the author had, but to embrace the issue and determine for themselves how they choose to regard and deal with it in their lives.

Do you agree with the author's analyses and recommended manner of addressing it?

If so, explain how you will apply it in your specific life's circumstances.

If not, please elaborate on how you view the issue and how you plan to address it as you live out the rest of your life.

What wisdom would you desire your children to receive from you on this issue to better prepare and equip them to deal with it in a truthful and God-honoring manner?

House Rules and Parental Guidelines
Letter 14

Proverbs 22:6
⁶ Start children off on the way they should go, and even when they are old they will not turn from it.

Matthew 18:6
⁶ "If anyone causes one of these little ones—those who believe in me—to stumble, it would be better for them to have a large millstone hung around their neck and to be drowned in the depths of the sea.

Dear David,

There are several aspects to the raising and nurturing of children that I have or will write about, and many others that you will have to deal with as this aspect of your life further unfolds. I want however to focus in this letter upon another aspect of this broad topic. It is best to understand this and implement it in your family while your daughters are younger, in preparation for their pre-adolescent and adolescent years. Its proper presence in your family will also help your daughters become more responsible and self-actualizing adults. The subject of this letter is "House Rules and Parental Guidelines."

I encourage you and Judy to spend time thinking and discussing what areas you would identify as your family's "core tenets." These are those aspects of life that define your family, that are integral to its identity and on which compromise would change the very fabric of what you believe your family should be. These are the areas you should desire for your daughters to adopt as their own and reflect in their adult life. These are the foundational principles and the infrastructure for your family upon which all decisions, choices, and priorities are built. They should be so important and deeply embraced that you are willing to sacrifice whatever is required for them to exist and flourish. These should arise out of Biblical truths; they are established "in stone" by you the caretakers of God's gift of children. They are to be regarded as non-negotiable in the eyes of your children. (Away from your children's presence, you as parents should be in continual dialogue to be certain that you have chosen the proper core tenets and assess how they are being enacted in and accepted by the family.) These core tenants should be few in number and have been shown in the lives of others over time to provide a solid foundation that will encourage a life lived for the benefit of God and man. They should undergird the daily life choices of the family as a unit and each person in the unit.

Arising out of and driven by these core tenets are what could be termed "household rules." These are strongly embraced and fairly rigidly enforced regulations that are to be recognized and accepted by all members of the family. Although parents will hear objections from the children and comparisons made to "other families," these rules are not to be regarded as optional. To violate them would challenge the core tenets out of which they have arisen; this would undermine the security and stability of the family. Although children

67

press for laxity and self-determination (they get to make the rules), they need the stability and solidness within their family that such rules create. Again, these rules should be carefully determined by the parents to be sure they are necessary to effectively uphold the core tenets. Do not make rules in order to secure personal power or fulfill some ego needs; they are not to be used to force your child into a specific mold that reflects your life choices or preferences. Even if a certain way of living worked for you it may not be the only way that a life can be lived upholding the core values. Think about your choice for these rules from various perspectives and discuss your intentions, relative to them, with older and wiser people. Once these rules are established, they should not be significantly altered or manipulated. Examples of such household rules could be: Respect toward others in the family, absence of harmful substances, responsible driving, worship on Sundays, obedience to school and other civic authorities, or the use of clean and honoring speech. I have found that household rules either are not ever established or, if established, not known or acknowledged by the family members, and are rarely or inconsistently enforced. Most children or teens can not name the Household rules of their family.

Beyond these "rules" are what could be termed "parental-family guidelines." These are directives, strong advice, urged considerations, experientially advocated choices, logical and sensible determinations, or Biblically demonstrated (but not dogmatic) ways of godly living. They can be linked to circumstances and will vary with the age or developmental stage of the young person. They may also vary between people based on their personalities, areas of vulnerability, peer influences, needs and desires. There can be some negotiation in the establishment of such guidelines, allowing input and conversation between parent and child. One person described these as "leash extenders" – they allow the young person to encounter life and to make (within flexible parameters) decisions for themselves and to chart their course in life. We, as parents, should discuss their choices with them and help them to weigh options. Guidelines should be agreed upon by both child and parents after a time of seeking input and prayer; they should not be made impulsively or driven by peer pressure. The decisions that you and your child make on guideline issues will be accompanied by the expectation that the child will be held responsible for the outcome of that decision for them individually, or for others inside or outside of the family. The goal is to teach your child responsibility and accountability. This process of identifying these guidelines and then implementing them, I have found, brings an atmosphere of intimacy, trust and unity to the household. Also, at times, implementing the chosen guidelines as a family brings opportunities for fun and adventure. The dynamic establishment and use of guidelines will lessen the tendency for conflict and rebellion, especially in the teen years. They will break the often-held image of parents "always saying No"; I urge parents to say "yes" in various ways and degrees to most guideline issues. Finally, the proper balance of rules and guidelines will provide a model and experiential teaching that can be reproduced by these children in their own families in the years to come.

David, this aspect of child raising blends the need to establish and maintain the family identity you seek while providing an environment that encourages and enables your child to be all that God desires for them.

Love,
David

Questions

Obviously in normal life one does not have the advantage to be able to evaluate and direct their life choices with the knowledge of their future. However, the author has in these letters created such a context to press each of us to focus on specific "life issues" proactively and intentionally in our younger years so that we, as we go forward, can direct our lives toward the best of all outcomes. These general questions should be regarded as a guide for the reader, individually or as a part of a small group, to address the issue at hand and make appropriate life decisions and choices.

What is the specific "life issue" the author is concerned about in this letter?

Why does the author feel this is an important issue to bring to a person's attention in their younger years; do you agree?

How did the author seem to deal with it as a younger man? Was his means of addressing the issue done properly or improperly, consciously or subconsciously, constructively or destructively, God honoring or man honoring?

How is the author, now as an older man, recommending that the specific issue be thought about and actively addressed?

The goal of each letter is not to convince the reader to deal with the issue as the author had, but to embrace the issue and determine for themselves how they choose to regard and deal with it in their lives.

Do you agree with the author's analyses and recommended manner of addressing it?

If so, explain how you will apply it in your specific life's circumstances.

If not, please elaborate on how you view the issue and how you plan to address it as you live out the rest of your life.

What wisdom would you desire your children to receive from you on this issue to better prepare and equip them to deal with it in a truthful and God-honoring manner?

Friends for Your Child
Letter 15

1 Corinthians 10:23
23 "I have the right to do anything," you say—but not everything is beneficial. "I have the right to do anything"—but not everything is constructive.

2 Timothy 2:22
22 Flee the evil desires of youth and pursue righteousness, faith, love and peace, along with those who call on the Lord out of a pure heart.

Proverbs 12:26, 18:24
26 The righteous choose their friends carefully, but the way of the wicked leads them astray.

24 One who has unreliable friends soon comes to ruin, but there is a friend who sticks closer than a brother.

Dear David,

Relative to the general subject of raising and nurturing children to be strong, effective and contented men or women of God, I want to suggest another critical area that you should attend to as a father. I have chosen to write you separately on this aspect of child raising because it is a crucial area. It is crucial because unless you actively address it, the world will address it for you and the results will be out of your control. It is crucial also because it can positively or negatively affect the inner person and character of your evolving young person as they move into adulthood. The presence of this area is a "given" in their life; it is a sure reality that can be a wonderfully positive force or source of great destruction. You must harness it for the good of your child and for God's Kingdom.

This critical area I am speaking about is your child's "friends." Peer interaction is inevitable and human; we are relational beings. Especially for children, who and what we are or become is influenced majorly by the explicit and implicit feedback from peers journeying on a similar path as ourselves. The reality is also that most people (even at young ages) embrace the standards of this depraved and fallen world and will transmit or impress them upon others that they relate to in friendships. Opposing this is a Biblical standard of beliefs, choices, and behaviors that should ideally reflect a positive evolving relationship between a person and God. The friends you desire for your child will reflect such a relationship and the behaviors it fosters. There, of course, are gradations and permeations of these two opposing ethical views at play in a given individual or relative to a specific issue at hand. For the child, the degree of influence their friends will have on their choices and actions become more clearly apparent and observable as they progress into adolescence and adulthood. Often, the child will give a parent a brief and informal opportunity to give their input into their choice of friends and the extent of their relationship with them but will reject in-depth discussion and any even remotely judgmental comments from a parent. They view this area as "theirs" and not the province of parental influence.

For every child the sociologic need for and validation from friends is a critical, almost desperate force. Although parents should continually be giving input on their child's choice of friends and their interaction with them, this input is often regarded as "old fashion" and designed (in the child's mind) to rob them of fun! Parental advice and recommendations are therefore suspect and held at arm's length. Although the child strongly seeks to retain this part of their life as their exclusive property, they do not recognize that they do not yet have the knowledge or experience to make life-giving (rather that life-destructive) decisions. This, parenthetically, is a tool the enemy (Satan) has used since the beginning of creation: to convince every person that they are their own authority and do not need to be under the "lordship" of anyone else, even their creator God. Therefore, the friends your child chooses and spends time with have more sway, often, than any adult. Teachers might be an exclusion here; they can occasionally be seen by the young person as being more neutral and less personally controlling.

The challenge and area of required attention then, David, is to engage your child, at the earliest age you can, in the proper seeking out of friends who are at least open to the input of God 's Word and His ethic. You will misjudge "potential friends" at times and could find yourself disappointed in the collaborative choices you and your child make. Even though you try to be proactive in this area, your child will often not seek your input and choose on their own friends you know nothing about. When you finally discover these selected friends, they may have already had a negative influence on your child. In reality, although you must try to help your child choose and build friendships with others, you are limited in your ability to accomplish this goal.

I recommend for your consideration these further thoughts on this friend issue. Firstly, encourage your child to have multiple friends (not a single or exclusive "best friend") and to interact together with others their age in a group. Within that group various relational dynamics and ethical options will be encountered and displayed; your child will have the opportunity to see the effect, both good and bad, of these in such a context. Also, there is safety within a group; he or she can afford to be rejected by a few as long as there are others that agree and support them in their perspective and behavior choices.

Secondly, try to steer your child's choice of a group (of peers) toward one that generally supports the values of your faith and family. Church youth groups (unfortunately these have recently fallen "suspect" by many youth), church related mission trips, and community sanctioned groups (e.g.: YMCA, Youth for Christ, work projects, or Scouts) are often places where like-minded parents are encouraging their young person's involvement. Also, sport's teams or music-oriented groups generally uphold good values and are intolerant of unethical behaviors or viewpoints. Whatever "group" your child is involved with, be aware that its leader is the most influential person in the group – this is (fortunately) usually an adult. Take the time to talk with them, find out about them and understand their goals and methodology for achieving these goals. They will be your surrogate for much of your child's time.

Thirdly, try to be a part of the organization and leadership of whatever group in which your child is involved. Do it as objectively and uncontrollably as possible; assume the attitude that you are there <u>along</u> with your son or daughter not <u>because</u> they are there. You might even originate and establish a group that would involve selected young people; this group would be built around some exciting and instructively valuable topic or interest. I especially like, if this is possible in your specific situation, bringing boys or girls (separate groups) together with several of the same gender parents to interact in various ways toward the goal of learning how to live as a man or woman of God in this world. This may seem to be too extreme or overt to your youth so you might have to settle for something like inviting several of their friends to join you (and maybe another parent) to work on a project, hobby, musical event or athletic related activity. Such things as building a tree house fortress, swimming lessons, weekend camping trips, biking excursions, cooking lessons, or community held garage sales could provide opportunities where the ethics of godliness can be comfortably shared, encouraged and demonstrated.

David, there may be many other ways you will determine as means to direct your daughter's need and desire for "friends." I admonish you to consider this and determine the best ways available to use this normal human need to help them grow safely and powerfully as a child of God in this hostile and potentially destructive world. Address this issue prayerfully and prioritize it at each level of their development.

Love,
David

Questions

Obviously in normal life one does not have the advantage to be able to evaluate and direct their life choices with the knowledge of their future. However, the author has in these letters created such a context to press each of us to focus on specific "life issues" proactively and intentionally in our younger years so that we, as we go forward, can direct our lives toward the best of all outcomes. These general questions should be regarded as a guide for the reader, individually or as a part of a small group, to address the issue at hand and make appropriate life decisions and choices.

What is the specific "life issue" the author is concerned about in this letter?

Why does the author feel this is an important issue to bring to a person's attention in their younger years; do you agree?

How did the author seem to deal with it as a younger man? Was his means of addressing the issue done properly or improperly, consciously or subconsciously, constructively or destructively, God honoring or man honoring?

How is the author, now as an older man, recommending that the specific issue be thought about and actively addressed?

The goal of each letter is not to convince the reader to deal with the issue as the author had, but to embrace the issue and determine for themselves how they choose to regard and deal with it in their lives.

Do you agree with the author's analyses and recommended manner of addressing it?

If so, explain how you will apply it in your specific life's circumstances.

If not, please elaborate on how you view the issue and how you plan to address it as you live out the rest of your life.

What wisdom would you desire your children to receive from you on this issue to better prepare and equip them to deal with it in a truthful and God-honoring manner?

Part 3
Faith Issues

Studying God's Word
Letter 16

2 Timothy 3:16-17
16 All Scripture is God-breathed and is useful for teaching, rebuking, correcting and training in righteousness, 17 so that the servant of God may be thoroughly equipped for every good work.

Hebrews 4:12
12 For the word of God is alive and active. Sharper than any double-edged sword, it penetrates even to dividing soul and spirit, joints and marrow; it judges the thoughts and attitudes of the heart.

Dear David,

Knowledge is important in order to live properly and to achieve the goals you have and will establish in this life. Obviously, you could not be prepared or permitted to practice medicine until you have demonstrated a competent knowledge of the profession. Even the ability to pursue non-professional interests or utilize tools for work around the home require an acquisition of knowledge. To have knowledge begins with reading or receiving verbal instruction from another who is more proficient than you in the subject and then advance that knowledge with "on the job" learning as you apply this "book learning" to real life situations. As you apply knowledge practically your deficiencies will be revealed, and you will recognize areas where you need further instruction. You will then be motivated to seek a further and deeper understanding that will lead to progressive proficiency. Learning is a dynamic and progressive pursuit and requires time, intent, perseverance, discipline and a willingness to "fail a bit" in the process. Learning should be regarded as a proper aspect of human living and has no age cut-off. It is both humbling and gratifying. It is essential if one is to be powerful and effective in any given area of their choice.

Knowledge of God's Word and spiritual learning is not an exception, although most people are content to have at best only a rudimentary knowledge of God and the truth found in His Word. Even for "church-going Christians" (as distinguished from non-believers on the one hand and dynamic disciples of Christ on the other hand) the knowledge of the Bible is said to be at a "fifth grade level." Yet these same people often view themselves as authoritative and knowledgeable enough to arrogantly judge the merits of God; they usually regard Him, though, incorrectly and incompletely. God is made to fit into <u>their</u> human world view and in this way they, in fact, make themselves their own god. I have even encountered people who call themselves "ministers of the Word" but behind this disguise, they pick and choose from the Bible what appeals to them or satiates some human need or aspiration. Others corrupt the Word by making it into a humanistic philosophy that offends no one and appears on the surface to be "caring" toward our fellow man. But behind these superficial but humanly acceptable fronts lie destructive self-serving motives and priorities.

Additionally, many people can easily be deceived and follow charismatic self-serving leaders; they might willingly give themselves and their wealth to false and misleading "religious cults." Such leaders do not represent accurately Biblical truth; such truths have long since been rejected, if ever known.

There, then, are two problems that surface relative to this topic of Biblical knowledge. Firstly, as I have just explained, ungodly people with self-serving motives can take your mind captive and distort truth and so disfigure God that He and truth are unrecognizable. Secondly, people have given up on seeking, or have never learned to seek, true knowledge and understanding from the Word. Further, they have not sought instruction from true disciples of Christ who speak or write about God in order to enable others to understand and apply His Word. It is this second area in which I want to admonish you.

There is no substitute for, or short cuts around, spending time studying God's Word, the Bible. I am not talking about just reading it through as part of your quiet time or focusing on a verse or two that surface in a morning devotional. "Church goers "equate the verses of Scripture read on Sunday morning as part of the Pastor's sermon or in the liturgy of the service as their effort in the Word. Often people, when asked about their study of the Word, offer these examples as their participation in this area. Although these have merit, they are limited in their ability to transform our soul. You must sequentially (at least within a given book from the Bible) read every verse, understand it within its context, integrate it into the fullness of the entire council of God and seek to understand the intent and background of the writer of that particular book. Explore key words, even to the point of understanding these words or phrases in their original language; enhance your study with an understanding of the geography of where it takes place or from where it was written; seek to place it properly in its historical setting. Be familiar with the sociological, philosophical and ethical perspectives of both the writer and the original readers. Allow your mind and your soul time to ponder what is being taught and modeled in that portion of His Word. You should, in prayer (before you even open the Bible), ask God through His Holy Spirit to open your heart and mind to what He wants you to learn or understand. Then discipline yourself to find opportunities in your daily life to apply or implement what He has taught you in your study.

The process will at times be difficult, demanding and overwhelming; you will have periods of being perplexed, discouraged, confused, and frustrated. The Word will create within you humility and bring you to a righteous fear of a just and powerful God. But as you do these things you will experience a greater joy, peace, excitement and hope than anything else this world can offer. The proper study of Scripture will enlarge and redefine your view of life, bring it more and more convergent with God's view, and open up possibilities for new and more powerful ways to use this acquired truth. You, through your study, will come to discover the spiritual gift He has given, or will give, you as the means to serve Him in His Kingdom.

It is important to study His Word using commentaries from solid Christian thinkers or be instructed by those who have already been applying His Word and therefore are regarded as credible teachers. You must, however, be cautious here; be sure what you read has been found to reflect true Christianity and the authors have been tried and proven as knowledgeable and accurate to the Word. Such study aids are of considerable help and value in your learning but, if not from credible sources, can cause a destructive influence.

Also, books written from a Christian perspective on life's topics can be stretching, offer good "food for thought" and compel you to assess your life and consider changes or new directions. But be sure they, as well, are coming from a solid Biblical foundation and have been accredited by others (scholars and Christian friends) who have read them. I encourage you to be reading at least one such book at all times in conjunction with pure Bible study (with or without commentaries).

Lastly, I have found that teaching God's Word, in any of a variety of scenarios, has been exceedingly helpful to me in this area of learning. For me, the study I do in preparation to teach others will force me to deeply scrutinize the Word and extensively seek cross references from other areas within the Word and from solid commentaries. Often, I will try to understand its meaning from the original Hebrew or Greek. Be careful as you assume the role of teacher; the enemy will desire to tempt you to become proud in your position as the "expert and teacher." Build humility into your teaching; be honest and transparent concerning the journey you have had to take in order to be able to teach them. Further, be willing yourself to sit at the feet of people more learned then yourself; be a teachable student. Finally, be willing and anxious to mentor others as they seek to be teachers themselves, especially those in younger generations. Some of the best times of learning for me have been in preparing myself to disciple another person, especially a daughter or a grandchild. (Note, even the telling of bedtime Bible stories requires proper study and preparation; an awesome opportunity!)

David, hear these exhortations and spend the rest of your life learning.

Love,
David

Questions

Obviously in normal life one does not have the advantage to be able to evaluate and direct their life choices with the knowledge of their future. However, the author has in these letters created such a context to press each of us to focus on specific "life issues" proactively and intentionally in our younger years so that we, as we go forward, can direct our lives toward the best of all outcomes. These general questions should be regarded as a guide for the reader, individually or as a part of a small group, to address the issue at hand and make appropriate life decisions and choices.

What is the specific "life issue" the author is concerned about in this letter?

Why does the author feel this is an important issue to bring to a person's attention in their younger years; do you agree?

How did the author seem to deal with it as a younger man? Was his means of addressing the issue done properly or improperly, consciously or subconsciously, constructively or destructively, God honoring or man honoring?

How is the author, now as an older man, recommending that the specific issue be thought about and actively addressed?

The goal of each letter is not to convince the reader to deal with the issue as the author had, but to embrace the issue and determine for themselves how they choose to regard and deal with it in their lives.

Do you agree with the author's analyses and recommended manner of addressing it?

If so, explain how you will apply it in your specific life's circumstances.

If not, please elaborate on how you view the issue and how you plan to address it as you live out the rest of your life.

What wisdom would you desire your children to receive from you on this issue to better prepare and equip them to deal with it in a truthful and God-honoring manner?

Praying and Journaling
Letter 17

Philippians 4:6
⁶ Do not be anxious about anything, but in every situation, by prayer and petition, with thanksgiving, present your requests to God.

Romans 8:26-27, 34
²⁶ In the same way, the Spirit helps us in our weakness. We do not know what we ought to pray for, but the Spirit himself intercedes for us through wordless groans. ²⁷ And he who searches our hearts knows the mind of the Spirit, because the Spirit intercedes for God's people in accordance with the will of God.

³⁴ Who then is the one who condemns? No one. Christ Jesus who died—more than that, who was raised to life—is at the right hand of God and is also interceding for us.

Numbers 33:1-2
¹Here are the stages in the journey of the Israelites when they came out of Egypt by divisions under the leadership of Moses and Aaron. ² At the Lord's command Moses recorded the stages in their journey.

Exodus 13:14-16
¹⁴ "In days to come, when your son asks you, 'What does this mean?' say to him, 'With a mighty hand the Lord brought us out of Egypt, out of the land of slavery. ¹⁵ When Pharaoh stubbornly refused to let us go, the Lord killed the firstborn of both people and animals in Egypt. This is why I sacrifice to the Lord the first male offspring of every womb and redeem each of my firstborn sons.' ¹⁶ And it will be like a sign on your hand and a symbol on your forehead that the Lord brought us out of Egypt with his mighty hand."

Dear David,

This letter will consider two spiritual disciplines in which people will not naturally do well unless they are committed to making an intentional and preemptive effort toward addressing them. The first step in accomplishing that which does not come naturally to us humanly is to become aware of the issue and its potential benefit to a person. Then, secondly, one should determine the obstacles in their life that deter them from its implementation. The purpose, then, of this letter is to motivate you to recognize and implement the practices of prayer and journaling.

Let's begin with the practice of prayer. I know you are praying and in fact are probably doing a better job in this area than most believers. However, this is such a crucially valuable and powerful aspect of being able to live powerfully in the Kingdom of God that you must progressively grow in it as you move forward through life. I admit immediately that this is a discipline that requires commitment and effort. Although there are practical and logistic considerations that impact our prayer life, I believe there are two fundamental obstacles that oppose and suppress our efforts to pray effectively. Although as Christians we find this hard to admit, most people, if they are honest, simply are not convinced that God hears and answers prayers. If we are not truly convinced of this then we will find it easy to embrace a weak prayer life; we allow ourselves to use lack of time, tiredness or life's demands as our excuse as to why we don't have a robust prayer life. Our experience in human relationships has taught us and accustomed us to the reality that people generally do not listen attentively and empathetically (see letter 3), even those who avow to love us and care about us. Further, we have also learned through experience that we cannot count on or depend on people to stand with us or to actively help us in a time of need. Now since this experientially derived perspective concerns people who we <u>can</u> see, hear and touch, we will find it even harder to functionally believe that God, who cannot be proven or authenticated by our human senses, will hear us or can be relied upon to answer prayers. Although, often out of a sense of guilt or routine, we make a superficial and somewhat mindless effort to pray, we have little confidence that we are being truly heard or that anything will come of our prayers. Additionally, without this confidence we will not have spiritual eyes and ears that are open and able to see or hear that indeed God has heard and is acting.

A second obstacle to a powerful prayer life is that most people, even professed believers, do not know the character of God and do not seek to know and follow His will. Therefore, even if we pray believing He hears and can act in our life in response to our prayers, we ask Him to act or intervene in ways that are contrary to His character or will. Humanly we would not ask another person to act in a way that would be contrary to their character or contrary to their fundamental goals and priorities. We would not ask this of them <u>because</u> we know them. A trusting faith in a God who listens and will act <u>according to His character and will</u> arises and grows out of an increasing knowledge about Him from our study of Scripture and from others who share with us their experiences with Him. Additionally, as we begin to see the evidence of an effective prayer life, we will confirm and testify to His character and that His will is "good, perfect and pleasing." Too often, though, we want Him to intervene in our lives as <u>we</u> (as myopic humans) <u>want</u> and <u>when</u> we want. We desire to be "in control" and arrogantly bully Him to "fall in line" with what <u>we</u> know is best. And if we don't get what we want we attribute it to Him being distant to us and powerlessness to act on our behalf. Really what we need is to be more "teachable" or "moldable" to His will and purposes by permitting His wisdom to change, modify or expand what we think and want.

Our regenerated spiritual nature battles our old flesh nature – the nature that influences us to live controlled by the sin of seeking to be our own god. Out of the context of this condition we are offended by and reject having to seek and rely upon God to orchestrate and direct our life. Then, when our blinded spiritual eyes do not allow us to see accomplished those things for which we have prayed, we default to our flesh wisdom and efforts; we take charge and control of our life, confirming in our inner person that we should rely on ourselves and not on God. Further, the enemy will reinforce this flesh perspective through the words of unbelieving people who will delight in reminding you that "God is dead;" they will encourage you to rely <u>only</u> upon yourself.

There are indeed many logistic and pragmatic issues that deter us from this discipline of faithful prayer. Time constraints, body-mind fatigue, illness, family demands, commitments (even to the church,) work overload and emotional stress are all realities of the human existence that can easily supply "reasonable excuses" for a weak prayer life. However, I believe these logistic realities can be minimalized if one addresses actively the two fundamental obstacles discussed above.

Related to the topic of effective praying is the issue of "fasting." I will not explore this extensively in this letter, but I would endorse the concept that sacrificing human comfort as we enter into prayer does create a climate that prepares and promotes us to be willing to trust Him and look to Him for true life and provision.

The second area that I wish to address in this letter is that of journaling. Like many other Christians, the thought of implementing the discipline of journaling immediately brings forth a resistance and a guilt fueled feeling of "yet another burden to accomplish." I hear you say: "I don't have time for that, I'm not good at writing things down," or "I agree that this is useful, but I have more crucial areas of my walk with God that I need to work on first!" I understand and hear you clearly. However, I have come to realize that journaling is a powerful way to get to know God and to build your faith. In fact, I know of no greater means to grow in your ability to trust God with increasingly more and more aspects of your life than through keeping a journal. Journaling is simply writing down how you see God acting in your life and how He has chosen to answer your prayers. To plan to place an entry into a journal at the end of each day will make you live that day with your eyes and ears open to how God has "shown up" or creatively answered your prayers. You will live more sensitized to His daily intervention. As you write down these wonderful experiences and revelations, your heart will leap as your mind acknowledges His powerful reality. When you go through spiritual "dry times," you can refresh your soul and savor His goodness all over again as you re-read your previous journal entries. Journaling, when shared, can be a powerful tool to teach and demonstrate to your maturing daughters the dynamic and "living" nature of our Lord. I believe we experience miracles, large and small, regularly, but may not recognize them because we are not looking and listening for them. Journaling tends to encourage us to keep our senses alert to His miracles.

David, I encourage you to consider these points, pray about them, discuss them with Judy and then set a course of action to address them. Do not expect this to be easy; you will wrestle with God and the enemy on these, because they are so important. Begin in a small but doable way and then be expecting and willing to grow in both your prayer life and in journaling; He will lead you and empower you in these areas as you make the human effort.

Love,
David

Questions

Obviously in normal life one does not have the advantage to be able to evaluate and direct their life choices with the knowledge of their future. However, the author has in these letters created such a context to press each of us to focus on specific "life issues" proactively and intentionally in our younger years so that we, as we go forward, can direct our lives toward the best of all outcomes. These general questions should be regarded as a guide for the reader, individually or as a part of a small group, to address the issue at hand and make appropriate life decisions and choices.

What is the specific "life issue" the author is concerned about in this letter?

Why does the author feel this is an important issue to bring to a person's attention in their younger years; do you agree?

How did the author seem to deal with it as a younger man? Was his means of addressing the issue done properly or improperly, consciously or subconsciously, constructively or destructively, God honoring or man honoring?

How is the author, now as an older man, recommending that the specific issue be thought about and actively addressed?

The goal of each letter is not to convince the reader to deal with the issue as the author had, but to embrace the issue and determine for themselves how they choose to regard and deal with it in their lives.

Do you agree with the author's analyses and recommended manner of addressing it?

If so, explain how you will apply it in your specific life's circumstances.

If not, please elaborate on how you view the issue and how you plan to address it as you live out the rest of your life.

What wisdom would you desire your children to receive from you on this issue to better prepare and equip them to deal with it in a truthful and God-honoring manner?

Hearing God

Letter 18

1 Kings 19:11-13
[11] The Lord said, "Go out and stand on the mountain in the presence of the Lord, for the Lord is about to pass by."
Then a great and powerful wind tore the mountains apart and shattered the rocks before the Lord, but the Lord was not in the wind. After the wind there was an earthquake, but the Lord was not in the earthquake. [12] After the earthquake came a fire, but the Lord was not in the fire. And after the fire came a gentle whisper. [13] When Elijah heard it, he pulled his cloak over his face and went out and stood at the mouth of the cave.
Then a voice said to him, "What are you doing here, Elijah?"

I Corinthians 2:9-10
[9] However, as it is written: "What no eye has seen, what no ear has heard, and what no human mind has conceived"—the things God has prepared for those who love him—
[10] these are the things God has revealed to us by his Spirit.
The Spirit searches all things, even the deep things of God.

Dear David,

This letter will step away from the dense and complex topics of the last few letters. Although easier to receive and understand, I think this topic is very crucial to Christian living and not well understood by believers. Yet it is taught and demonstrated clearly in the Word. I write about "hearing God in our lives."

Many people, as they move from childhood to adulthood, possess only a simple and rudimentary knowledge of God; often our childhood view of God and the biblical stories we heard in Sunday School remain even into our adult years. For instance, God the Father is often thus viewed as big, powerful, determined and distant; Jesus however is viewed as soft, kind and docile. However, as we acquire a greater and more accurate knowledge of God and understanding of His Word, these immature views should be replaced by a truer concept of the Father, Son and Holy Spirit.

One of these retained childhood views of God is that when (or if) He appears or speaks to people He does so in powerful and easily recognized ways. We look for obvious and dramatic miracles as the evidence of God's intervention. We listen for the loud clear voice of God in our prayers and we seek to hear in the counsel of our friends or mentors the unmistakable wisdom of God. We also look to the natural world for physical evidence, unexplainable by scientific reasoning, that God is present and speaking to us. (see 1 Kings 19:9b-12). Do not misunderstand me, I do believe God does and can work in these more overt, obvious and dramatic ways, but He is not to be limited to these. He often speaks and acts more subtly, softly and indirectly; to hear or see Him requires informed and prepared eyes and ears. He is way more creative, diverse and all-encompassing than to be limited by our immature human view of how He expresses Himself in people's lives. He is sovereign over all creation, all circumstances and time. Although He will act as a result of His deep unconditional love, His actions are expressed in a manner directed by His wisdom, will and sovereign control.

We begin to better understand how to hear God by first firmly believing that God hears and answers prayers; He deeply desires to answer the prayers of His faithful but must do so according to His will (see Letter 17). The Scripture tells us that Jesus is at the right hand of the Father interceding on our behalf and that the Holy Spirit speaks for us when we do not know what to pray (Romans 8:26-27, 8:34). With this well understood then we communicate in prayer what we need or desire. We speak honestly and transparently but realize that He is God and must act as God. Too often, however, we ask in prayer for God to act according to our wisdom and then look for that specific answer – expecting it to be just like what we asked for and at the time we asked for it to be accomplished. As humans we want to define how God is to interact with His followers; we want to put Him in a box, limiting Him to our meager human possibilities; we see Him as a vending machine, dispensing at our demand. We must instead, after we pray to a God big enough and creative enough to answer according to His wisdom and love, wait expectantly and in confidence for the response – a response that may be immediate or delayed or may be according to our choices or consistent with His better choice. His response also may be heard or received loudly and in easily recognizable ways or in soft, subtle, not easily recognizable ways. In my experience God more often than not is seen and heard in subtle ways.

Therefore, we must develop eyes to see and ears to hear God as He speaks to us in His Word, in nature, through the casual words of others, in everyday events, in the little miracles, or in the silence of our soul as we pray. There have been only a few times I can say that I heard the very words of God spoken, not audibly but clearly, within the depth of my being. More often He speaks through the nonverbal movement of the Spirit that brings me to know or understand His mind or heart. To hear God, therefore, one has to consistently and regularly seek times of being apart from the world and desiring God; in this posture their soul can be attuned to God so that they can receive His critically important and life directing communications.

We must train ourselves, as we walk through our daily lives, to evaluate each event or interaction as being a possible message or response from God. However, it is easy to begin to read into these situations what really isn't from God, so be sure to seek prayerful and Scriptural confirmation that what you hear, or experience, is really from Him. At times there may be several events or interactions that are closely sequenced together such that it provides us an even greater certainty that what we are hearing is authentically from God. Be particularly alert to the words from other mature believers; God often, in my experience, informs me of His will and direction through them. Most often those who bring me His counsel do so unaware that they are His spokesman; only rarely, in my experience, has He brought to me a person who is overtly aware and affirms to me that they are conveying His message: in the role of a prophet. God has, in my experience, used at times the rest of His creation, birds and stars especially, to affirm or clarify His response to my seeking. These occurrences are powerful and beautiful but again can be easily overlooked or entirely missed.

Usually His Word (the Scripture) is where I hear and see Him, where I am admonished and exhorted, how I am trained and disciplined, and where His character becomes further known to me. This is a powerful reason that motivates me to eagerly read and study His Word daily and discerningly (see letter 16). I have come to the point in my life that I am frightened to even consider going a day without feeding on His Word. This, I believe, is His chosen means for speaking to and preparing His servants. Yet again we must approach scripture expectantly with eyes and ears wide open to receive His specific counsel to us for our daily life.

"God is dead" has been a banner for the evil unbelieving world in its attack upon our Creator. David, nothing could be further from the truth: God is very much alive and actively involved in the lives of those who believe in and seek Him. However, we need to hear God in all His chosen ways, many of which require us to listen more carefully and adjust our eyes to see Him in our world. What an amazing adventure and journey.

Love,
David

Questions

Obviously in normal life one does not have the advantage to be able to evaluate and direct their life choices with the knowledge of their future. However, the author has in these letters created such a context to press each of us to focus on specific "life issues" proactively and intentionally in our younger years so that we, as we go forward, can direct our lives toward the best of all outcomes. These general questions should be regarded as a guide for the reader, individually or as a part of a small group, to address the issue at hand and make appropriate life decisions and choices.

What is the specific "life issue" the author is concerned about in this letter?

Why does the author feel this is an important issue to bring to a person's attention in their younger years; do you agree?

How did the author seem to deal with it as a younger man? Was his means of addressing the issue done properly or improperly, consciously or subconsciously, constructively or destructively, God honoring or man honoring?

How is the author, now as an older man, recommending that the specific issue be thought about and actively addressed?

The goal of each letter is not to convince the reader to deal with the issue as the author had, but to embrace the issue and determine for themselves how they choose to regard and deal with it in their lives.

Do you agree with the author's analyses and recommended manner of addressing it?

If so, explain how you will apply it in your specific life's circumstances.

If not, please elaborate on how you view the issue and how you plan to address it as you live out the rest of your life.

What wisdom would you desire your children to receive from you on this issue to better prepare and equip them to deal with it in a truthful and God-honoring manner?

Sabbath
Letter 19

Hebrews 4:9-11
⁹ There remains, then, a Sabbath-rest for the people of God; ¹⁰ for anyone who enters God's rest also rests from their works, just as God did from his. ¹¹ Let us, therefore, make every effort to enter that rest, so that no one will perish by following their example of disobedience.

Mark 2:27-28
²⁷ Then he said to them, "The Sabbath was made for man, not man for the Sabbath. ²⁸ So the Son of Man is Lord even of the Sabbath."

Exodus 20:11
¹¹ For in six days the Lord made the heavens and the earth, the sea, and all that is in them, but he rested on the seventh day. Therefore the Lord blessed the Sabbath day and made it holy.

Dear David,

You have been taught to have a strong work ethic. More significantly than that is that you were raised to equate your value or worth as a person to your productivity: both in amount and in the quality of your work. You learned to be efficient with the use of your time and to prioritize goal accomplishment rather than developing the creative and abstract part of your mind, relationships, leisure pursuits and spiritual dimensions. You were taught to organize your life in such a way that you could assign a relatively small part of time and effort into these aspects of your life. You achieved an acceptable balance in your life as judged by societal or the world's measures and could well be labeled "successful."

There are many downsides, I have come to understand, that result from this world-view and the life choices it produces. In this letter, I want to focus on one negative result that often is overlooked. I want to call your attention to how you keep the Sabbath. You have arrived at the place in your life where you, in your effort to be productive and time efficient, have minimized the importance and time spent in the pursuit of spiritual growth and worship activities. You have selfishly protected your time and energy and restricted your Sabbath activities in order to not take away from the "more essential things" of your world. Looking back, your childhood experience of the Sabbath was fashioned loosely around the traditional view of it: a time for morning church attendance and then the rest of the day was set aside as a time to rest your body and pursue enjoyable leisure activities. Perhaps, a Sunday would also include a larger family centered dinner, visits to relatives, a walk outside, or doing an activity where all members of the immediate family would participate. In our modern world to today even these features of a Sabbath Sunday have begun to wane as our fast paced, highly technological, self-serving, and pleasure-seeking priorities have crowded out this "old time" approach to the Sabbath. Although seeking to keep ourselves away from

94

work (anything that is measurable in terms of productivity) and to intentionally focus on rest and relationships are positive and a movement in the proper direction, it misses God's intent for us relative to how we keep His Sabbath.

God had intended, after He had completed His work of creation, that His whole creation would live eternally in His Sabbath rest. Yes, man was to carry out the activity of having dominion over all of creation (in some sense this can be seen as work), but this was accompanied by peace and a deep satisfaction as we acted as God's representatives and His "image bearer." As man resided in this Sabbath rest, he would be in continuous fellowship with Him, our creator, and could enjoy Him as He in turn enjoyed His creation, especially mankind. It was His intention that we would grow daily in our knowledge and understanding of Him and delight in a deepening love relationship with Him as we dwelled in His presence. This was the Shalom or "Rest" that God had in mind for us. Shalom is that state of our being that can exist when all that God has created is functioning in the perfectly balanced and complete manner He intended. With the fall, all this was lost; it will only be fully achieved again someday when Christ returns and restores the "Eden" that was lost by sin. Only then will His intention for creation, the holy "Rest" (Genesis 2:1-3), be enjoyed forever.

But now during the church age, when we live in the "Spiritual Kingdom," we must define how we can appropriately seek and enjoy some degree of this intended unity and fellowship with God. At best, most professed Christians allocate a few hours Sunday morning to a church experience – defined by the evolving sociologic interpretation of "church." (See letter 21) But this participation is mostly passive and distant; we have delegated worship to the few while the rest of those in the pews take on a spectator role. In the worship services of modern America, I have very rarely experienced myself, or known of too many others, who have enjoyed the fellowship of our God and therein been soulfully restored or have experienced His promised peace (shalom) during this time of corporate worship. The remainder of our Sunday is spent in work around the home, preparation for school or the upcoming work week, self-satisfying human leisure activities or the obligatory (but often stressed) family interactions. This is the usual modern American Sabbath.

What would it look like if you really spent an entire Sabbath Sunday in spiritual endeavors that brought growth in our knowledge of our God and a fresh and fuller anointing of His Spirit? Would this allow us to experience a deeper peace and joy: His Shalom, His "Holy Rest?" I am not suggesting a reclusive, self-denying, martyr-type existence each Sunday, but I exhort you to brainstorm creatively how a proper Sabbath would look for you and the family. It must start, I believe, from a position that rejects the world's definition of Sunday, and then seeks to allow the Spirit to instruct you in His desire for how you are to experience Him and fellowship with Him. I expect that there would be some similarities but also significant individualization amongst true believers. I don't think God has a singular prescribed way of relating to Him any more than deep friendships between people would all appear the same. I think it would be exciting and fun to explore with your wife and young family how to use and enjoy your day of rest and spiritual refreshment.

Be aware though, David, that such an endeavor may require tough choices relative to other opportunities and demands upon your family's life. Many activities in today's world are scheduled on Sunday; to keep the Sabbath properly may mean denying members of your family the option of participating in these activities. Your friends, how you view work and your leisure activities or hobbies, the importance of possessions and property, your habits, and areas of temptations can all be affected by how you redefine your Sabbath. In fact, if at least some of these areas are not impacted then I suspect you have not accomplished the goals of this exhortation. All of life will be impacted by the proper use of God's Sabbath.

You must understand this issue, pray about it, and discuss it with your spiritual mentors and your family. Then proactively change how you use your Sunday so you will receive what will otherwise be lost. God will surely bless you as you live in His peace.

Love,
David

Questions

Obviously in normal life one does not have the advantage to be able to evaluate and direct their life choices with the knowledge of their future. However, the author has in these letters created such a context to press each of us to focus on specific "life issues" proactively and intentionally in our younger years so that we, as we go forward, can direct our lives toward the best of all outcomes. These general questions should be regarded as a guide for the reader, individually or as a part of a small group, to address the issue at hand and make appropriate life decisions and choices.

What is the specific "life issue" the author is concerned about in this letter?

Why does the author feel this is an important issue to bring to a person's attention in their younger years; do you agree?

How did the author seem to deal with it as a younger man? Was his means of addressing the issue done properly or improperly, consciously or subconsciously, constructively or destructively, God honoring or man honoring?

How is the author, now as an older man, recommending that the specific issue be thought about and actively addressed?

The goal of each letter is not to convince the reader to deal with the issue as the author had, but to embrace the issue and determine for themselves how they choose to regard and deal with it in their lives.

Do you agree with the author's analyses and recommended manner of addressing it?

If so, explain how you will apply it in your specific life's circumstances.

If not, please elaborate on how you view the issue and how you plan to address it as you live out the rest of your life.

What wisdom would you desire your children to receive from you on this issue to better prepare and equip them to deal with it in a truthful and God-honoring manner?

Discipling
Letter 20

Galatians 1:18-19
¹⁸ Then after three years, I went up to Jerusalem to get acquainted with Cephas and stayed with him fifteen days. ¹⁹ I saw none of the other apostles—only James, the Lord's brother.

Acts 18:24-26
²⁴ Meanwhile a Jew named Apollos, a native of Alexandria, came to Ephesus. He was a learned man, with a thorough knowledge of the Scriptures. ²⁵ He had been instructed in the way of the Lord, and he spoke with great fervor and taught about Jesus accurately, though he knew only the baptism of John. ²⁶ He began to speak boldly in the synagogue. When Priscilla and Aquila heard him, they invited him to their home and explained to him the way of God more adequately.

2 Timothy 1:13-14
¹³ What you heard from me, keep as the pattern of sound teaching, with faith and love in Christ Jesus. ¹⁴ Guard the good deposit that was entrusted to you—guard it with the help of the Holy Spirit who lives in us.

Dear David,

You are in a very demanding and busy time of your life; there are multiple opportunities, responsibilities and life choices that pervade your daily schedule. You are escalating your professional activities, building the marriage and growing your family; you have a home that requires work and attention and hobbies that appeal to your human side. It is easy to put the non-pressing things of your spiritual growth as a low priority; since the world devalues these there is no external reward for effort in this area. Drifting along with God is what usually occurs; we offer Him one or two hours on Sunday morning and maybe a bit of time participating in the affairs of the local church. The truth is, though, there is no such thing as remaining static (or drifting) in your spiritual life – if you are not growing and seeing progressive transformation (becoming more like Christ!) then you will decline, grow cold and progressively move toward forgetting God.

I must admonish you to intentionally and proactively devise and execute a plan that will ensure growth and maturation rather than decline and rejection of God. Although individual or private Bible study and prayer is essential, and worship with a believing community required, there is another avenue that I will direct you to pursue. This falls under the category of "discipleship:" to be trained and to train others to build the Kingdom of God.

The process of being discipled by another begins firstly with you humbly and honestly assessing your present level of spiritual maturity and what you desire your spiritual life to become. You must seek to discern God's will for you and set reasonable goals for yourself so that you accomplish properly His will for you (see letter 1). The main component in this process is the consistent and active meeting together of two men, one who is viewed as being more spiritually mature, and another who seeks to grow in his walk with Christ. To be "discipled" you must seek God's leading to identify the man who will be your discipler and then take the steps necessary to implement it. Both of you must share this calling (toward discipleship) as a result of your individual relationships with the Lord. You both must work hard to carve out the time to meet regularly and both (especially the one being mentored) must do what is agreed upon in preparation for each meeting. The place to meet must be found; a place that permits freedom to speak candidly and to pray together. David, as you are being "discipled" be warned that you may start out with enthusiasm but unless you discipline yourself toward this effort you will not persevere but begin to find excuses why you cannot meet or are unprepared. In this you will need the Lord's resolve and strength. The enemy will desire to destroy this powerful pillar of Kingdom work. You may ask: "How long should I be discipled?" the answer is forever! There will never be a time that you are unable to learn from and be molded by a wiser and more godly man.

Concurrently to you being discipled is your need, as well as your privilege, to disciple another man who is younger in his walk than yourself. The first precaution you must confront as one who disciples another is that this role must not serve to inflate your ego - if that happens, you will fail in your efforts on behalf of this other man. Helpful in preventing this human tendency is, as I described above, being discipled yourself; this acts to balance how we view ourselves. Begin by praying that God will lead you to that person who He desires you to relate to as His agent for their growth and transformation. Be alert to His choice and be ready to accept the challenge. Engage this man in every meeting with commitment, perseverance, honesty and effort; this is hard work and you will be challenged in it by society, human frailty (his and yours) and the direct assault by the enemy. Realize your efforts may at times seem fruitless, as if you are spinning your wheels; at times you will be emotionally negative to these interactions as well. But you must be willing (as he also must be) to be in it for the long haul. Confront together with integrity the obstacles that will war against this discipling dynamic.

These relationships of discipleship will be amongst the strongest, most real, most beneficial and most enjoyable dynamics you will ever experience in your life. They are precious treasures that must be sought after and guarded. You are indeed standing on holy ground as you relate in this manner: God is deeply pleased as you walk this road.

The Godhead is the perfect discipling community and the relationship between the Father, the Son and the Holy Spirit is vibrant, satisfying, edifying and the source of "completeness" for each. Since we are made in His image, we also must seek and develop such relationships. God will be with you and bless you as you are being discipled and as you disciple another.

Love,
David

Questions

Obviously in normal life one does not have the advantage to be able to evaluate and direct their life choices with the knowledge of their future. However, the author has in these letters created such a context to press each of us to focus on specific "life issues" proactively and intentionally in our younger years so that we, as we go forward, can direct our lives toward the best of all outcomes. These general questions should be regarded as a guide for the reader, individually or as a part of a small group, to address the issue at hand and make appropriate life decisions and choices.

What is the specific "life issue" the author is concerned about in this letter?

Why does the author feel this is an important issue to bring to a person's attention in their younger years; do you agree?

How did the author seem to deal with it as a younger man? Was his means of addressing the issue done properly or improperly, consciously or subconsciously, constructively or destructively, God honoring or man honoring?

How is the author, now as an older man, recommending that the specific issue be thought about and actively addressed?

The goal of each letter is not to convince the reader to deal with the issue as the author had, but to embrace the issue and determine for themselves how they choose to regard and deal with it in their lives.

Do you agree with the author's analyses and recommended manner of addressing it?

If so, explain how you will apply it in your specific life's circumstances.

If not, please elaborate on how you view the issue and how you plan to address it as you live out the rest of your life.

What wisdom would you desire your children to receive from you on this issue to better prepare and equip them to deal with it in a truthful and God-honoring manner?

The Local Church

Letter 21

Acts 2:42-47
⁴² They devoted themselves to the apostles' teaching and to fellowship, to the breaking of bread and to prayer. ⁴³ Everyone was filled with awe at the many wonders and signs performed by the apostles. ⁴⁴ All the believers were together and had everything in common. ⁴⁵ They sold property and possessions to give to anyone who had need. ⁴⁶ Every day they continued to meet together in the temple courts. They broke bread in their homes and ate together with glad and sincere hearts, ⁴⁷ praising God and enjoying the favor of all the people. And the Lord added to their number daily those who were being saved.

Colossians 3:15-16
¹⁵ Let the peace of Christ rule in your hearts, since as members of one body you were called to peace. And be thankful. ¹⁶ Let the message of Christ dwell among you richly as you teach and admonish one another with all wisdom through psalms, hymns, and songs from the Spirit, singing to God with gratitude in your hearts.

Dear David,

This letter is a difficult one to write, yet there is much that needs to be said on this topic. I do not pretend to have arrived at a full understanding of the subject nor am I convinced that what I am about to say is the only right perspective. I might indeed have written something a bit different if I had written this letter two years ago or would write it two years from now. But I am compelled to pass on to you what I have learned about this subject to date so that it might benefit you as you and your family go forward. The subject of this letter is the "local Church."

I remember as a teenager pondering (with a very limited knowledge base) the value of "going to church" or being a part of an organization called church. I suspect most young people grapple with this issue. Yet in reality my youthful ponderings were, in retrospect, just a cover up in an effort to justify my human flesh desire not be involved in a local church. To make this justification exercise even more tempting and achievable was the fact that my parents basically felt negative to the church and so did not oppose my rejecting stance. Thankfully God had other plans for me, and I came to a personal confession of faith at age 13 at a church camp. No longer could I justify my non-involvement in the church, the Body of Christ.

The local enactment of Christ's Body, the local church, has since its inception been a source of controversy and conflict, a crucible and battle ground for opposing theological values, priorities and practices. It also has been, and can be, a powerful force for Christ or, at times, a destructive tool of the enemy. It is easy for people to find reason to criticize it or participate in it only superficially as a social club or humanitarian organization. Although this is the reality of the situation, the local church is God's chosen method and means to bring

His Gospel to the world. The truth is: everyone who defines themselves as a Christian is part of His body and must be actively involved in a local church for growth and service. There are no exceptions or excuses.

That now understood, David, you must lead your family in this endeavor. Here are some aspects of a local church that I have come to understand and exhort you to consider:

#1. The church must value and adhere to the whole counsel of God: The Biblical Word. It's teachings at all levels, its decisions, its structure and administration, the relationships between the members, and its interface with the non-believing world must be defined and directed by the truth of the Word. The teaching and preaching should not be done with human wisdom but by the insight and revelation of the Holy Spirit. The Word should, for the most part, be expositional rather than topically presented. The teacher or preacher should not "proof-text" the Scripture by extracting verses out of their Biblical context but deal with verses sequentially as they are presented in the Word. They must be willing to wrestle with the difficult and controversial verses, as well as the comfortable ones, as they are encountered in the Scripture. Humility must characterize the teacher as he or she approaches the Word and brings it to the listeners. Proper study and preparation are required of the teacher; sufficient time must be set aside so that the Word dwells within the expositor before he or she speaks in order that its meaning may be progressively revealed to them by the Spirit. I prefer that the Word be presented in such a way that the listeners can, to some degree, interact with the teacher and share with the gathered body insights they also are receiving from the Spirit. The Word, in this way, is more likely to be understood as God intends and allows all those present to have ownership of it. Mutual ownership will encourage and enable all in the local body to then apply it in their lives. Contributions from the listeners, especially if they are encouraged to also prepare and study beforehand, will help keep the teacher humble and be a great incentive for the teacher to seriously seek the Lord in their preparation and presentation.

#2. Seek a church that recognizes and embraces the core dogma of our faith. The leadership should aggressively and passionately guard its sanctity and seek to make sure all who attend embrace it as absolute truth. Dogma truths are clearly defined in the Word, are relatively few in number, and should be agreed upon by all members. There are, beyond this foundational core dogma, many areas of Christian concerns and practices that are not clearly dogma but fall more into the area of doctrine. These are areas of Scripture that can be interpreted in more than one way and are not essential to the faith. Also, God has in some cases not yet clearly spoken on how to understand some aspects of spiritual reality and its application to daily living. Doctrinal differences have often been the cause of division, conflict and ungodly behavior within the local church. Numerous denominations have formed as a result of difference in doctrine, and, sadly, painful church splits that result in damaged relationships and spiritual disillusionment have been, and continue to be, the result of too much focus on doctrinal differences and variations. The result, relative to God's Kingdom, is the weakening of the Body's ability to serve Him and the unattractive and counterproductive testimony it displays to an unbelieving world. We must learn humility, respect, patience and forbearance (Eph. 4:1-6) for one another, and trust that the Spirit would indwell the dynamics within the body to foster growth and discipleship.

#3. The number of people (the size of the church) who defined themselves as a particular local church family is a factor important to its ability to accomplish its goals. Although the "mega church" concept has merit as an evangelical means of bringing Christ to the modern world, I believe much that is truly part of God's intent for the local church can be lost in such a church structure.

There is a variable balance relative to what is the proper number of people who regularly worship and serve together: there must be enough people who are committed to each other and regularly gather in order to accomplish the necessary aspects of church life and purpose, yet not so many that any given person and their needs are not well known. Some aspects of corporate worship are enriched by a sufficient number of people. Also, the presence, availability and utilization of the Spiritual gifts required for the edification of fellow believers need a sufficient number of people who gather regularly as a body. Additionally, the church's specific means for outreach and community service are accomplishable with a given (but not fixed) number of workers. However, if the committed gathered are too many then intimacy in prayer and fellowship is less achievable. The number of people who gather as the church should be small enough that every person can be "known" in the depth of their person so that each can be properly discipled. Lesser numbers in the body will allow human needs to be assessed and met more fully as the members feel the freedom to be transparent and vulnerable. To discover your spiritual gifts requires that people know you deeply and relate frequently with you. Full participation in worship and the ability to interact with the teacher during the message is also made more likely with smaller numbers. It is easier to get "lost" in the crowds and to silently "pull back" from worship or ministry involvement when the numbers are larger.

I seriously question that these same goals, purposes, and dynamics can be accomplished through "small groups" within a larger congregation. It is an important responsibility of church leaders to continually seek to know how God would have the members properly discipled and shepherded, and then to effectively implement this in the life of every person in the body. Without this continual Spirit-directed leadership the local church will succumb to the enemy and will fall far short of God's will. If the primary means within a church for disciple building is in "small groups" then this responsibility falls upon the person leading each group. If each person leading a group is not fully in step with the Spirit, then I fear too much reliance on human effort will take place and proper discipleship will not sufficiently succeed. Realistically, to have a successful "small group ministry" the church must find and develop people to be able to also clearly "hear" the Spirit and then be able to edify others to grow and serve. I have yet to see this effectively accomplished, appropriate to the standards of the Scriptures, through the process of small groups.

As to what is the proper number of people in a local church, I am not able to say. This, I believe, will vary significantly and ultimately the Spirit will determine this for any given church. Every congregation should continually seek this in prayer, listening to the Lord. I am inclined toward the number of 75-200 people.

My last comment, relative to church size, is that there should be a point when a given body, after becoming too large to meet the goals stated above, must divide into two smaller churches. This step is humanly uncomfortable and will be met, understandably, with resistance. Although these smaller churches may come together on occasion for larger corporate worship, the majority of the life and service intended by God for believers would exist within and arise out of each of these smaller bodies.

#4. Every local church should seek the Spirit's leading to define their specific outreach ministries. Christ, in John 14:15, states that "If you love me you will obey my teaching!" Christ taught and His life exemplified sacrificial, "other-focused" love as He reached out to others without regard to who they were humanly. Therefore, as a natural and expected result of each member growing as a disciple, they too will, in obedience to the Gospel, reach out in sacrificial love to their community. Evangelism toward the nonbeliever in the community is best accomplished through personal relationships as each believer demonstrates this agape (sacrificial) love for others. Also, serving others requires the church to meet the tangible, emotional and relational needs of those living in this broken world right in their community. The members of the local church can, further, be led by the Spirit to reach out to other places in the United States or internationally. Some in the church may even be called and commissioned as "missionaries" while others are called to support them with prayer and resources. This outreach aspect of the local church should be ever present in its mentality and always at the forefront of its prayers and decisions. The body must listen to the Spirit's leading and be willing to move ahead in dynamic service, often in faith and a trustful reliance on His provision.

#5. Important to the dynamics and work of the local church is the acquisition and use of financial resources. The majority of monies given in faith to the church should be used for ministry; only a small part for building rent, salary and internal program support. The accomplishment of service efforts and outreach should be the primary focus for our giving. As people grow in personal discipleship, they will be encouraged by the Spirit to contribute money toward the church's ministry, at times even to a level that requires sacrifice: "sacrificial giving." Such giving is counter-cultural and opposes the self-seeking philosophies of the world. However, members must accept this uncomfortable challenge, because it is scripturally "right" and edifying to their growth as disciples. God can choose to bless a person in some way as they give sacrificially, although this should not be the motivation for giving. Each family within the local church should participate in this process of financial stewardship.

#6. I have come to believe that the local church should not be solely led by a single "Head (or lead) pastor" but that leadership must be shared by several "pastor-elders." As a team they will be able to know the will of the Spirit more fully and accurately, and balance one another's humanity. Team leadership encourages and ensures some degree of humility and accountability – necessary but often lacking areas within church leadership. Within that pastor-elder group each person will utilize their gifts, strengths and experiences to accomplish specific needs or goals. For instance, two or more of them may fulfill the teacher-preacher role, whereas another might be gifted and trained in areas of shepherding. It is permissible to provide a salary to one or more of them depending on their family's need, the time they will be required to invest, and their educational and experiential background. This pastor-elder arrangement is a challenge to our human-flesh nature at several levels and the default direction has been traditionally toward the "professional clergy" model. Therefore, to implement such a leadership structure may require these leaders to honestly confront some deeply seated personal needs and emotions. It is also important to educate the entire body on this model and help them to learn how to best use their elders and what they should expect from them as leaders. They will probably have not experienced this leadership style before.

As a further balance within this leadership model and to keep the church Biblically solid, I advocate the selection and active utilization of a person to serve in an "apostle (or evangelist) role." This person is not a part of that particular local church but is knowledgeable and solidly grounded in the Word and has had experience in developing elder-led local churches. The local body and the elders should pray that God will provide such a person; seek them out and use them to advise, admonish, exhort, discipline and teach the elder-pastors of the church.

#7. De-emphasize the physical building in which you meet. A building is not the church; the people led by Christ are the church. Have sufficient room to accommodate whatever number ends up in your church family and allows you to accomplish the internal needs and goals of your church. The space should be regarded as "holy" and conducive to powerful worship, fellowship and discipleship. Facility provisions for youth and children should be considered. Be willing to change the location as God leads and your church evolves. Try not to invest much money or resources into a physical structure or human conveniences; it can easily become self-serving.

#8. Integrate, as much as possible, your youth and children into all aspects of your church life. Involve the older youth to help plan worship, participate in outreach projects, choose teaching topics and help plan fellowship events. Use their gifts and talents and seek their input on most church matters. Be sure they are being discipled by some adult or more mature older youth.

Allow the children to be in the entire service (with maybe an occasional exception) and incorporate into the worship service meaningful learning and worship opportunities for them. Ignore their restlessness, crying, "out of the blue" comments, and disruptive behaviors; do not let these deter worship or the teaching of the Word. These are to be expected from children and need not be an obstacle for us adults; view them instead as a blessing. Jesus had strong words to say about how we are to regard children and He encouraged their entrance and participation in His Kingdom. Overlook their "non-adult" behavior and show excitement to them, and for them, as they dwell in your midst. They learn much by just being in your presence, even if it is not obvious to you.

It may be reasonable to establish specific events or teaching for teenagers, children or young adults, but these should be additive to and not a replacement of inclusive corporate church worship. They should exist to achieve a defined purpose identified and sought by the body at large. Do everything possible to keep the church family together in unity and love; we are all part of Christ's Body.

#9. The proper and healthy local church elevates and delights in Holy Communion. It should be a highlight of the worship services; the frequency is not fixed in Scripture, so seek this through the Spirit's wisdom. Consider an expanded teaching and instruction concerning communion that would accompany the act of taking the elements. It should be recognized as both a personal and corporate sacrament; it gives life to our individual and collective souls. In the participation of Holy Communion, the body should experience a sense of unity and love. It is a mysterious and powerful celebration, one that is indwelled by the Holy Spirit. It is an awesome privilege we have been given. Respect it, honor it and love it.

#10. Finally, be part of a local church that seeks actively to relate to and act in concert with the other local non-church entities in your community. We must be strong in our internal unity but if we keep ourselves separate from, or at odds with, the greater community in which we live then we miss the opportunity to be a powerful force for Christ's Kingdom. The church which, in the view of non-believers, is seen as separated from the world, internally conflictual, or antagonistic to the culture will confirm their belief that Christianity is "not for them." Such an analysis and opinion from the community onlookers only adds fuel for Satan's effort to destroy God's plan for building His Kingdom.

Yes, I agree, this is a long and detailed letter but an important one. Please read, ponder, talk about it with others and make intentional decisions to achieve for Christ the purpose for which His church was called into being.

Love,
David

Questions

Obviously in normal life one does not have the advantage to be able to evaluate and direct their life choices with the knowledge of their future. However, the author has in these letters created such a context to press each of us to focus on specific "life issues" proactively and intentionally in our younger years so that we, as we go forward, can direct our lives toward the best of all outcomes. These general questions should be regarded as a guide for the reader, individually or as a part of a small group, to address the issue at hand and make appropriate life decisions and choices.

What is the specific "life issue" the author is concerned about in this letter?

Why does the author feel this is an important issue to bring to a person's attention in their younger years; do you agree?

How did the author seem to deal with it as a younger man? Was his means of addressing the issue done properly or improperly, consciously or subconsciously, constructively or destructively, God honoring or man honoring?

How is the author, now as an older man, recommending that the specific issue be thought about and actively addressed?

The goal of each letter is not to convince the reader to deal with the issue as the author had, but to embrace the issue and determine for themselves how they choose to regard and deal with it in their lives.

Do you agree with the author's analyses and recommended manner of addressing it?

If so, explain how you will apply it in your specific life's circumstances.

If not, please elaborate on how you view the issue and how you plan to address it as you live out the rest of your life.

What wisdom would you desire your children to receive from you on this issue to better prepare and equip them to deal with it in a truthful and God-honoring manner?

Part 4
Principles and Concerns

Materialism

Letter 22

1 John 2:15-17
15 Do not love the world or anything in the world. If anyone loves the world, love for the Father is not in them. 16 For everything in the world—the lust of the flesh, the lust of the eyes, and the pride of life—comes not from the Father but from the world. 17 The world and its desires pass away, but whoever does the will of God lives forever.

Dear David,

It's nearly Christmas as I am writing this letter. I am surrounded in our home by gifts – so many that it covers a quarter of the floor space in our family room. The market places of our community appeal to our greed nature and, in many clever ways, seeks to convince us that we "need" and "can't live without" material things. We are a consumer society; we gauge our value and pleasure on what we possess; our identity as a person is defined and equated to what we own and how well we live. Unless you recognize this situation and the destructive consequences it can have upon you and your family, you will find yourself amongst the crowds that walk this broad and enticing materialistic road! This letter is written in the hope that you might recognize the problem and then build into your choices and life style a different journey.

It is easy to understand how we have arrived at this sad and joy-robbing place. As part of the flesh nature (the consequence of original sin) we seek to build an empire around ourselves as its king. With this comes the pressure to live as a king in wealth and comfort, and to be recognized by others for our high status. Large homes, expensive cars, luxury vacations, the finest of clothes, excessive furnishings and home décor items, the newest and best "electronics," and expansive "collections" (of all sorts) are features of our Western human society. This worldview is modeled, taught and expected as we move through childhood to adulthood. The higher our worldly status and the more we possess, the more influence we have (good and bad) on others and the more temptations of the flesh we will encounter. Yet we read and hear daily of the tragic end and depraved lives of those who, by whatever means, have "arrived at the top." There is, therefore, a large price-tag for materialism and a life of acquisition. The cost can be, for example, the destruction of one's moral fiber and healthy relationships, or a life characterized by fear and anxiety. Such a life will bring with it a pressure to work even harder and longer, a desensitization to proper ethical and legal parameters, a progressive and encompassing unrest and joylessness, and an inability to serve God in His Kingdom. It is, in fact, very difficult to really know God and prioritize serving Him (as a part of the Body of Christ) while pursuing such dictates and directives of the world.

My parent's and grandparent's generation emerged from the "Great Depression" where survival alone was the daily task; acquiring things was only possible for the very wealthy and financially conniving of the population: the rich got richer and the poor got poorer. A positive offshoot of that situation was the need to and willingness to work hard and sacrifice whatever was required to benefit the family. As the economy improved and people sought to buy things as a way to not feel the pain of "living without," their strong work ethic and self-sacrifice was channeled into efforts to seek possessions and obtain human comfort. Technology advancing at an unbelievable pace made this goal achievable and attractive; people were easily drawn into acquiring devices and machines that made life easier and allowed more free time.

Free time and available money also brought forth a mentality of "collecting and vacationing." These two areas, I believe, reflect the pinnacle of materialism. Collecting (of which I have been guilty of!) is the acquiring of a particular type of a thing just for the sake of having it; those who have the biggest and best collection are really seeking peer valuation and recognition. Also, in this their human flesh may experience a fleeting and transient pleasure. They often are willing to sacrifice family needs, time and emotional energy to simply acquire yet another thing for the collection. Relative to the issue of vacations, people are willing to work long and hard, disregarding or deprioritizing other (more important) aspects of their family's life in order to save and plan for vacations and vacation homes. Progressively they seek bigger, better and more luxurious trips and retreats from their usual daily life. This cycle of saving for and spending on vacationing tends to result in an enslaving vicious cycle: work hard to spend more and work harder yet to spend even more. The pressure to acquire and "have" results in an escalating background of worry and anxiety; we fear that we will not make enough money to achieve our consumer goals or that someone else will outshine us and reduce our materialism generated self-worth. I confess that I have been drawn into this materialism and thing acquisition mentality slowly and progressively because I was not understanding of its "trap" and God's better perspective on it.

The Bible is clear on this subject. God exhorts us to discipline ourselves to trust Him to provide all that we need to live. As we learn to trust Him, the enslaving treadmill of human acquisition and peer approval melts away; it loses its ability to drive us into the despair generated by self-seeking priorities. Further, as we seek God and trust Him for our provision, we will progressively know Him better, spend more time in the Word and in prayer, and discover amazing opportunities to minister to other people. The fear and anxiety that accompanies the "human way" is replaced with a deep joy and peace as we seek God's provision and the Holy Spirit's wisdom, counsel and comfort. Time that we would have spent consumed by materialism would now be available to properly nurture our family, disciple others and give to the truly needy in our community. Also, and very importantly, how we deal with this issue of materialism will mold and instruct the next generations: children and grandchildren. Their future and the future work of the Kingdom of God is at stake here. It requires your serious consideration.

Now, I do not wish to motivate you by guilt, so I remind you that God understands, forgives and is powerful to change our human tendencies. If this direction in your life has already taken hold, it is now time to re-assess and proactively, with God, consider changes. He will lead you.

Finally, I believe God does understand the human desire for comfort and things of the created world. He often will allow us to enjoy these things; blessings that reduce the pain and oppression of the world. I refer you to consider His promises to His people, Israel, in Deuteronomy 28:1-14. Yet it is clear from Scripture that material things are not the central desire God has for His people; His desire is that we "seek Him and His Kingdom" (Matthew 6:33-34) then He will provide all that, in His wisdom, we need. At times we could receive an abundance of created things but only, I believe, if in His wisdom these things will not distract from our seeking after Him. He is more concerned with our attitude and willingness to put Him and His Kingdom first in our life than He is to make sure we live comfortably in the world. There is no one level of living standard that connotes godly people and families; we are all unique and individual to God and He relates to us in this way. There will be differentiation amongst Christians relative to the acquisition of material things but common to all true believers is our need to devote ourselves to and trust God's call upon our life.

This, David, is a difficult balance to achieve; seek God, through the Word and prayer, for proper discernment.

Love,
David

Questions

Obviously in normal life one does not have the advantage to be able to evaluate and direct their life choices with the knowledge of their future. However, the author has in these letters created such a context to press each of us to focus on specific "life issues" proactively and intentionally in our younger years so that we, as we go forward, can direct our lives toward the best of all outcomes. These general questions should be regarded as a guide for the reader, individually or as a part of a small group, to address the issue at hand and make appropriate life decisions and choices.

What is the specific "life issue" the author is concerned about in this letter?

Why does the author feel this is an important issue to bring to a person's attention in their younger years; do you agree?

How did the author seem to deal with it as a younger man? Was his means of addressing the issue done properly or improperly, consciously or subconsciously, constructively or destructively, God honoring or man honoring?

How is the author, now as an older man, recommending that the specific issue be thought about and actively addressed?

The goal of each letter is not to convince the reader to deal with the issue as the author had, but to embrace the issue and determine for themselves how they choose to regard and deal with it in their lives.

Do you agree with the author's analyses and recommended manner of addressing it?

If so, explain how you will apply it in your specific life's circumstances.

If not, please elaborate on how you view the issue and how you plan to address it as you live out the rest of your life.

What wisdom would you desire your children to receive from you on this issue to better prepare and equip them to deal with it in a truthful and God-honoring manner?

Holiday Celebration

Letter 23

Isaiah 9:6-7

⁶ For to us a child is born, to us a son is given, and the government will be on his shoulders. And he will be called Wonderful Counselor, Mighty God, Everlasting Father, Prince of Peace. ⁷ Of the greatness of his government and peace there will be no end. He will reign on David's throne and over his kingdom, establishing and upholding it with justice and righteousness from that time on and forever. The zeal of the Lord Almighty will accomplish this.

Isaiah 53:3-5

³ He was despised and rejected by mankind, a man of suffering, and familiar with pain. Like one from whom people hide their faces He was despised, and we held him in low esteem. ⁴ Surely he took up our pain and bore our suffering, yet we considered him punished by God, stricken by him, and afflicted. ⁵ But he was pierced for our transgressions, he was crushed for our iniquities; the punishment that brought us peace was on him, and by his wounds we are healed.

Dear David,

Holidays, during my years growing up, were always special and (as I remember) almost magical. My home of origin was mostly a place of tension and unpredictability; an undercurrent of brewing conflict was frequently present. Yet with almost every holiday my mother loved to decorate in order to create an atmosphere that brought, for a short time, a reprieve from the tension; we felt a welcomed but fragile time of calmness. As kids we looked forward to these relatively elaborate and abundant times, compared to our rather bland and "bare-bones" daily existence. We enjoyed the special privileges afforded by holidays: gift giving, moments of laughter, traditional meals, and times with our extended family. But I think most of all we sought that coveted but temporary time of peace and security.

As Judy and you established your own home and traditions, you, without intending to do so, recreated to some extent the holiday times you both remembered from your childhood. Judy had, in her home growing up, similar positive holiday experiences but with a much more consistently secure and loving home environment. Thus, your developing family participated with delight in holiday decorating, preparing special food, choosing and purchasing gifts and spending intentional and quality time together to make a given holiday special and memorable. You sought for these occasions to be an intimate, family-focused time with your daughters; therefore, you were willing to cooperate with the world's definition of how to "keep the holidays!" This approach has its merits – there was laughter, wonderful food and sugary treats, new adventures, time doing games together as a family and gift exchanges at Christmas. Yet in this means of celebrating, you progressively lost sight of the true meaning of that special time and the proper purpose for celebrating the holiday. Often at the conclusion of the celebration you felt an uncomfortable disappointment and a vague but discernable sadness. Especially concerning was that during the celebration of Christmas and Easter, God was given only "lip-service," being acknowledged only briefly and superficially. Also, the original and greater purposes for other holidays were forgotten as well in the family's efforts to enjoy time off work and school and savor human pleasures. Additionally, you have observed that in the last several years Halloween has seemed to be gaining increasing interest and attention from our society. This trend has concerned you as you have become more sensitive to the issue of good and evil in this world. Valentine's Day also grew in popularity with its focus on the human, fleshly type of love.

Regrettably you let these cultural trends subtly gain influence in your home and were preparing your daughters, through your example, to continue this direction in their future families. Although you were aware to some degree of your "buy-in" to the world's ways, you were not aware sufficiently of this encroaching destructive trend and not spiritually strong enough to counter it. I write this letter to admonish you to seek to return your holiday celebrations back to a more God-glorifying time.

You, David, must look hard at why and how you are currently celebrating a given holiday; what are your goals in these celebrations (both for you as adults and parents, and also for your daughters); what specific choices must you make in order to accomplish your goals; what sociologic pressures will counter the celebration you seek to enact for your family in order to modify or replace the worldly one now embraced? The foundational criteria, as you re-evaluate holiday celebration, is this question: In your celebration, how are you recognizing and

honoring God, your country, and the blessings you enjoy as a family? Yet at the same time, your celebration should allow your family to have fun and to grow together through new adventures and activities.

A particular area for your reconsideration is the giving and receiving of gifts at Christmas. The whole process of buying gifts for one another in order to satiate material and self-serving flesh desires need to be examined afresh. Presents should serve to facilitate relationships between people and between each person and God. They should reflect a growing knowledge of the person we are giving to and reflect their specific character, talents and interests. Or said another way, these gifts should reflect our "other focused" love arising out of a growing knowledge of and relationship with this other. Giving might, even more appropriately, be to others outside the family or to a group or organization that your spirit leads you to consider. Families should pray and talk with one another to decide who outside of the family should receive their gift and what the gift would be. Of course, other parts of the Christmas celebration should also be evaluated seeking to be sure that each part advances or enhances the purpose and goal of the holiday: the celebration of the birth of the Christ.

Easter is another, and maybe even a more important, example. In today's world the celebrating of the passion of our Lord has deteriorated into a secular event. Sadly, it has become for most a secondary holiday (behind Halloween, often) and is most valued only as a sign of Springtime and nicer weather. Redefining how we celebrate Easter and elevating it to the high position it deserves must be done in your home. The Easter Bunny, colored eggs, candy and baked ham for dinner have to be reevaluated and their presence reconfigured so that they reflect the powerful event of Christ's resurrection. If they cannot do this, then they should be abandoned. The worship of our Lord should be central to this holiday.

There are many other challenges that await your attention; each holiday must be reviewed, honestly evaluated and a new, revised and properly focused means of celebrating it established. Do it as a family but you must, as a father, be accountable for the result. Your daughters will carry forward, in their own families, the critical decision and choices you make now in your family.

Holidays are special, David, but their celebration must be under your supervision, as you listen and respond to the Spirit in your life.

Love,
David

Questions

Obviously in normal life one does not have the advantage to be able to evaluate and direct their life choices with the knowledge of their future. However, the author has in these letters created such a context to press each of us to focus on specific "life issues" proactively and intentionally in our younger years so that we, as we go forward, can direct our lives toward the best of all outcomes. These general questions should be regarded as a guide for the reader, individually or as a part of a small group, to address the issue at hand and make appropriate life decisions and choices.

What is the specific "life issue" the author is concerned about in this letter?

Why does the author feel this is an important issue to bring to a person's attention in their younger years; do you agree?

How did the author seem to deal with it as a younger man? Was his means of addressing the issue done properly or improperly, consciously or subconsciously, constructively or destructively, God honoring or man honoring?

How is the author, now as an older man, recommending that the specific issue be thought about and actively addressed?

The goal of each letter is not to convince the reader to deal with the issue as the author had, but to embrace the issue and determine for themselves how they choose to regard and deal with it in their lives.

Do you agree with the author's analyses and recommended manner of addressing it?

If so, explain how you will apply it in your specific life's circumstances.

If not, please elaborate on how you view the issue and how you plan to address it as you live out the rest of your life.

What wisdom would you desire your children to receive from you on this issue to better prepare and equip them to deal with it in a truthful and God-honoring manner?

Sacrificial Giving
Letter 24

2 Corinthians 9:6-8
⁶ Remember this: Whoever sows sparingly will also reap sparingly, and whoever sows generously will also reap generously. ⁷ Each of you should give what you have decided in your heart to give, not reluctantly or under compulsion, for God loves a cheerful giver. ⁸ And God is able to bless you abundantly, so that in all things at all times, having all that you need, you will abound in every good work.

Philippians 2:5-8
⁵ In your relationships with one another, have the same mindset as Christ Jesus:
⁶ Who, being in very nature God, did not consider equality with God something to be used to his own advantage; ⁷rather, he made himself nothing by taking the very nature of a servant, being made in human likeness. ⁸And being found in appearance as a man, he humbled himself by becoming obedient to death – even death on a cross!

Dear David,

I need to discuss with you an aspect of your life that if not proactively addressed will limit your potential to live fully as a new creation in Christ. I would like to focus on the area of "sacrificial giving." As you stretch yourself to give this way to others you will know a unique blessing and be able to serve Him better in His Kingdom. Although I have alluded to this in several of my previous letters, I want to highlight it now because it is so central to our identity in Christ.

I grew up in a house where my father (the dominant authority that set the course for our family) was a product of the Great Depression in the 1930s. He had to strive hard and persevere through significant difficulties to raise himself up out of a low-income life style to a higher socio-economic status. However, this journey established a selfish perspective that pressed him to want to hold on to what he regarded as "his," the result of his hard work. It deterred him from giving to others; if giving didn't promise a greater return, it was not done. This philosophy coincided with a worldly approved and humanly understandable view that a person should "enjoy what you have earned." In truth it represented a veneer overlying a deep desire (common to all fallen humanity) to self-exalt and build our personal kingdom with ourselves as the king. Sin had found, again, a societally and humanly acceptable way of depriving one of a fulfilled life. In reality, and as time would prove, this robbed my father (and us as his family) of another opportunity to experience true joy and peace; it was a significant force that distorted and eventually poisoned his relationships to my mother and weakened the proper character development of his sons.

"Giving," if it is true giving, must involve sacrifice. Sacrificial giving is not natural to our fallen human condition, especially we who have grown up in this affluent Western culture. Often, we see demonstrated and embraced the reality that the more you have the more you want and the less generous you are with what you have. You, David, must break this pattern so that your life will know the unique blessing of giving sacrificially. Your relationships to your wife and daughters, those outside the family and those who you will deal with in your medical practice will be greatly impacted by this decision. The discipline of sacrificial giving is a manifestation of our new life "in Christ" that begins when you acknowledge and receive God's great sacrificial, love gift of His Son (see Philippians 2:6-8). Then, as God promises (see John 14:15-26), He sends the Holy Spirit who transforms us from that human flesh controlled and depraved state into this new creation. This new creation (progressively become more like Christ) will embrace a desire and choice to give sacrificially. As you are then enabled by the Spirit you must daily practice this discipline so that it becomes a habit of righteousness. You will find that it becomes easier to give in this manner as you experience the blessedness of this act: a unique and indescribable "inner glow." There is a deep satisfaction that comes when you sacrificially give to another. The more that other person is "not deserving" or "has not earned" your generosity, the more Christ-like your giving becomes. The more it hurts or feels like you are depriving yourself in your giving, the more honoring and pleasing it is to God.

I must explain here that I am not talking just about giving money or "tangible things," although that is certainly an appropriate part of giving. But also included in sacrificial giving is our investment in others of our time, our emotional support and care, discipling efforts and the teaching and training of others. Sacrificial giving will (and should) bring, each time you give, a moment of hesitancy as you realize, in your humanity, that in this giving you will reduce what you possess or take away from your self-serving storehouse (see Luke 12:13-21). Satan will want to deter your giving by urging you to protect "what is yours!" The more you practice this discipline the less you will sense the sting of this perceived human loss.

Progressively, as you become more and more Christ-like, you will grow in your willingness to give away all your possessions and all of your life for others. This is in fact what Jesus did for us. God doesn't often ask us to completely empty ourselves of the world or self, but we must be willing to do so if He asks. (I have known of people who have indeed sacrificed all for Him, at His request). He understands where we each are in this area; if we seek Him in this issue, He will lead us to take one step at a time as we learn to give sacrificially.

As I seek to "finish well" in this life I have come to know that sacrificial giving is what true godliness is all about. God truly desires for us to know the "blessedness of giving."

Contemplate these thoughts and take action today.

Love,
David

Questions

Obviously in normal life one does not have the advantage to be able to evaluate and direct their life choices with the knowledge of their future. However, the author has in these letters created such a context to press each of us to focus on specific "life issues" proactively and intentionally in our younger years so that we, as we go forward, can direct our lives toward the best of all outcomes. These general questions should be regarded as a guide for the reader, individually or as a part of a small group, to address the issue at hand and make appropriate life decisions and choices.

What is the specific "life issue" the author is concerned about in this letter?

Why does the author feel this is an important issue to bring to a person's attention in their younger years; do you agree?

How did the author seem to deal with it as a younger man? Was his means of addressing the issue done properly or improperly, consciously or subconsciously, constructively or destructively, God honoring or man honoring?

How is the author, now as an older man, recommending that the specific issue be thought about and actively addressed?

The goal of each letter is not to convince the reader to deal with the issue as the author had, but to embrace the issue and determine for themselves how they choose to regard and deal with it in their lives.

Do you agree with the author's analyses and recommended manner of addressing it?

If so, explain how you will apply it in your specific life's circumstances.

If not, please elaborate on how you view the issue and how you plan to address it as you live out the rest of your life.

What wisdom would you desire your children to receive from you on this issue to better prepare and equip them to deal with it in a truthful and God-honoring manner?

Regarding Women
Letter 25

Romans 12:10
^{10} Be devoted to one another in love. Honor one another above yourselves.

1 Corinthians 3:16-17
^{16} Don't you know that you yourselves are God's temple and that God's Spirit dwells in your midst? ^{17} If anyone destroys God's temple, God will destroy that person; for God's temple is sacred, and you together are that temple.

Colossians 3:12
^{12} Therefore, as God's chosen people, holy and dearly loved, clothe yourselves with compassion, kindness, humility, gentleness and patience.

Dear David,

As I have grown older, I have come to realize that I was raised in a male-dominated and paternalistic environment. The world my father built and inhabited held a high view of maleness. This world emphasized a male's responsibility to be an independent, strong, self-asserting, goal-directed, hard-working and resilient figure in his role in the family, his work and the community. Emotions, sensitivity, philosophizing, spirituality and relationships were de-emphasized or viewed as "feminine and soft."

With such a perspective I entered my adolescence and young adult years: a time, traditionally, when a young man begins to form a relationship with a woman. Unfortunately, as a predictable result of this distorted egocentric view of maleness came an equally distorted and harmful view of women. The marriages I observed placed the woman under the domination and subjective evaluation of a man, and her views, opinions and perspective were generally viewed as uninformed and disregarded. It is, based on this, easy to see how a young girl, a young adult female and a wife would feel disrespected, unappreciated and dishonored. Further, this imbalanced and destructive dynamic was often taught and modeled.

You entered marriage holding, at least to some degree, this distorted and unhealthy perspective. But God was at work causing you to begin to question it and to give yourself permission to go a different direction in your relationship. As your love for God and His Word developed, you began to see your wife, Judy, differently and with a fresh and humbled heart. She is an extraordinarily talented, intelligent, level-headed and capable person; indeed, in many regards much more so than you. It was difficult to deny your growing respect and admiration for her and thereby you felt the need to reevaluate and redefine your role as a husband. Concurrently you were developing an understanding of sacrificial and unconditional love; you were wrestling with how that should be applied in your marriage. Further, you observed a reversal in your marital relationship in a few areas that dismantled the traditional male-female roles. For instance, often it was you, not her, that was more sensitive, more romantic, more prone to reflection and more nurturing. Although you still sought to add to your family selected and healthy male traits, you no longer saw yourself as dominant or superior; you saw her as your equal, your best friend, your helpmate and your strength. Important also to your journey in this area was the fact that you began to have daughters to raise. You saw your daughters as unique and gifted people, equal to any man and not having to be restricted in what they could contribute; they were encouraged to strive to "do whatever they wanted to do in life." As time went on this was rephrased in your mind as: "They could do <u>whatever God</u> had called them and prepared them to do in life."

God created woman as a help mate to man to make both of them whole and fulfilled; He intended that together as a unit they would form the secure, solid foundation needed for the family. With this in mind I came to realize that to dishonor my wife and the mother of my children was to dishonor God Himself. Women have unique and specially created features intrinsic to that mysterious femaleness, just as men have in their maleness. It is God's amazing wisdom that brought into being this mutual dependency and blessedness. It is one of the most marvelous aspects of His creativeness and speaks loudly of His kindness. We must be continually thankful and give honor to the God of creation by honoring firstly our wives and then the other women we encounter in our day by day life. We must actively seek to counter society's pervasive view of seeing women as sexual objects or as people only there to meet our male needs. Our words and actions must be respectful, sensitive, encouraging and appreciative. As we work with and relate to females in our daily life, we must view them as equals and welcome their contributions and perspectives.

You must encourage young boys and young men to speak and act in a way that upholds and promotes the dignity and value of all people. They must intentionally choose to be different in their interactions with women - contrary to the pull of traditional human society. Remember, in Christ there is no male or female; we are new creations and we all have equal parts in His body. We need each other in order to serve Him well in His Kingdom.

Although the content of this letter, David, applies most specifically to you as a young man, I believe it is also important for young women to hear and embrace these thoughts as well. I strongly encourage young women to love themselves to such an extent that they will require men who relate to them to demonstrate honor and respect. Do not permit men who seek your company in the context of relationship, in the work place, or even in casual interactions, to depersonalize you, devalue you, take advantage of you, make you feel inferior, or seek to physically abuse or dominate you. You are not a sexual object that exists for their pleasure or gratification. You are a person of character and substance. You are a beautiful, valuable, honored child of God; live your life with this belief. When you do so you will find that the men in your life will quickly understand what you expect and require of them; although they many not verbalize it, they are aware that this is right and proper.

David, with this perspective well established you will be able to avoid many destructive consequences that could arise out of improper and ungodly interactions with females both in the home and in the world at large.

I love you,
David

Addendum:

Within this unbalanced and distorted view of maleness, "religion" and particularly relational Christianity was relegated to something that a true man should place low in his priorities and invest minimal time. I often reflect on my father's advice relative to my growing interest in the Bible and Christianity: "David, do not get too carried away with this; keep it in perspective!" What he meant was: Religion is to be regarded as a badge of a balanced man but should not be central to his identity. Do not accept such advice and perspective.

Questions

Obviously in normal life one does not have the advantage to be able to evaluate and direct their life choices with the knowledge of their future. However, the author has in these letters created such a context to press each of us to focus on specific "life issues" proactively and intentionally in our younger years so that we, as we go forward, can direct our lives toward the best of all outcomes. These general questions should be regarded as a guide for the reader, individually or as a part of a small group, to address the issue at hand and make appropriate life decisions and choices.

What is the specific "life issue" the author is concerned about in this letter?

Why does the author feel this is an important issue to bring to a person's attention in their younger years; do you agree?

How did the author seem to deal with it as a younger man? Was his means of addressing the issue done properly or improperly, consciously or subconsciously, constructively or destructively, God honoring or man honoring?

How is the author, now as an older man, recommending that the specific issue be thought about and actively addressed?

The goal of each letter is not to convince the reader to deal with the issue as the author had, but to embrace the issue and determine for themselves how they choose to regard and deal with it in their lives.

Do you agree with the author's analyses and recommended manner of addressing it?

If so, explain how you will apply it in your specific life's circumstances.

If not, please elaborate on how you view the issue and how you plan to address it as you live out the rest of your life.

What wisdom would you desire your children to receive from you on this issue to better prepare and equip them to deal with it in a truthful and God-honoring manner?

Caring for those in Need

Letter 26

James 2:14-17

14 What good is it, my brothers and sisters, if someone claims to have faith but has no deeds? Can such faith save them? 15 Suppose a brother or a sister is without clothes and daily food. 16 If one of you says to them, "Go in peace; keep warm and well fed," but does nothing about their physical needs, what good is it? 17 In the same way, faith by itself, if it is not accompanied by action, is dead.

Dear David,

As I reflect back over the years, I have become sadly aware of a "perspective of neglect and exclusion" that I have held. Although subtle, it has powerfully directed some of my attitudes and choices. Yes, I know that sounds judgmental, but these words portray my concern about this situation and my urging to alert you to this before it becomes too ingrained.

In an effort to work hard, achieve goals, provide for the family, carve out time for recreation and even participate actively in a local church, there has been little time or emotional energy left to consider reaching out to the poor and disadvantaged in your midst. You, like many people of advantage, had arranged your comfortable life such that you never encounter such people; if you do encounter them, your eyes have been so desensitized that you look past them and you "simply don't see them." Often, you are able to convince yourself that it is someone else's responsibility (or some social agency). You might even, in an effort to justify your avoidance, see those in need as "frightening or dangerous." Therefore, you rarely allow yourself to get close enough to realize that they, like us, are God's creation, uniquely formed and loved by Him. You don't spend enough time in their presence to understand their journey and the magnitude of their need. However, I am certain that the greatest need they, like us, have is to be known and cared about. If you don't intentionally plan and act to reach out to the needy, you and your children could live your entire lives separated from the very people Jesus exhorted His disciples to care for. In this neglect you dishonor Him and His teachings, you deny yourself of a source of great spiritual and human blessing and you perpetuate in your children this same degree of unkindness and insensitivity.

Certainly, one person or one family is limited in what they can do in this area, but any bit of involvement, tangible or relational, will be multiplied by God's unseen presence and power. If every true believer would give even a small amount of their time and resources, our poor and needy could be greatly and positively impacted. You need to decide as a family how to reach out, when and where you will contribute or serve, and to what extent. Then you must not let the inevitable demands of life get in your way of repetitively and persistently doing so; it should become a "family habit" and integral to your family identity. Those you are reaching out to may (probably will) seek to manipulate you to give more, or they may appear ungrateful. It is likely that people who have been abused and rejected by society will feel and act out of a deep-seated anger, resentment and disillusionment. It is your responsibility is to do what is right in God's eyes and according to Biblical teaching; their motives and response to your efforts is not your business and should not define or determine your conduct. It is God's business, not ours, to judge; our business is to give "sacrificially!"

There, that's the word: "Sacrificially!!" We must adopt the Godly perspective of loving and giving to those we view as unlovable or unworthy in such a way that we feel the sacrifice (see letter 24). It's really not giving unless we feel the sting of loss in some way as a result of giving to another. We must remember that we have life only because He gave sacrificially (Jesus' death), and any abundance in life we enjoy is by His choice and generosity; we did not "earn" anything. This counter-cultural and humanly irrational perspective cannot be generated out of the human mindset but will emerge only from a mind transformed by the Holy Spirit (Romans 12:2). That's where we start: we must be changed by His Spirit if we are to be an agent of change and sacrificial giving in this fallen world.

Consider, David, these thoughts before you and the family are too set in the ways of the world and calloused to the deep needs of those neglected and excluded.

Love,
David

Questions

Obviously in normal life one does not have the advantage to be able to evaluate and direct their life choices with the knowledge of their future. However, the author has in these letters created such a context to press each of us to focus on specific "life issues" proactively and intentionally in our younger years so that we, as we go forward, can direct our lives toward the best of all outcomes. These general questions should be regarded as a guide for the reader, individually or as a part of a small group, to address the issue at hand and make appropriate life decisions and choices.

What is the specific "life issue" the author is concerned about in this letter?

Why does the author feel this is an important issue to bring to a person's attention in their younger years; do you agree?

How did the author seem to deal with it as a younger man? Was his means of addressing the issue done properly or improperly, consciously or subconsciously, constructively or destructively, God honoring or man honoring?

How is the author, now as an older man, recommending that the specific issue be thought about and actively addressed?

The goal of each letter is not to convince the reader to deal with the issue as the author had, but to embrace the issue and determine for themselves how they choose to regard and deal with it in their lives.

Do you agree with the author's analyses and recommended manner of addressing it?

If so, explain how you will apply it in your specific life's circumstances.

If not, please elaborate on how you view the issue and how you plan to address it as you live out the rest of your life.

What wisdom would you desire your children to receive from you on this issue to better prepare and equip them to deal with it in a truthful and God-honoring manner?

Racial and Ethnic Differentiation
Letter 27

James 2:1-4
[1]My brothers and sisters, believers in our glorious Lord Jesus Christ must not show favoritism. [2]Suppose a man comes into your meeting wearing a gold ring and fine clothes, and a poor man in filthy old clothes also comes in. [3]If you show special attention to the man wearing fine clothes and say, "Here's a good seat for you," but say to the poor man, "You stand there" or "Sit on the floor by my feet," [4]have you not discriminated among yourselves and become judges with evil thoughts?

Galatians 3:26-28
[26]So in Christ Jesus you are all children of God through faith, [27]for all of you who were baptized into Christ have clothed yourselves with Christ. [28]There is neither Jew nor Gentile, neither slave nor free, nor is there male and female, for you are all one in Christ Jesus.

Dear David,

There are some topics I write to you about that I feel more knowledgeable and complete in my understanding then others. Relative to the ones I feel more lacking in, I suspect this is so because either I have not wrestled enough personally with the issue (usually because of less opportunity or lack of requirement), or that it is deeply complex (it escapes my, or anyone's, ability to fully comprehend). Additionally, I may not have confronted some deeply situated obstacle within me to allow me to openly hear truth and then make an intentional effort to grow in that specific area. In reality it is probably some combination of these factors that are at play in any particular area in which I have poorly dealt. Often there is appropriate and adequate Biblical teaching on any given topic or issue, but for multiple reasons I have not engaged these teachings and applied them. The issue of racial differentiation is one of these areas; I feel inadequate to explore the subject well. However, I write this letter about it because I want to admonish you to proactively, intentionally and honestly confront this area so that you will arrive at my age better able to act properly relative to it and teach the next generation more accurately the truth.

I view this subject as one that deeply concerns God and, more than many other aspects of humanity, is reflective of the fundamental sin of self-exaltation. Although every person is guilty of seeking to exalt self at the expense of others, racial bias as a cultural manifestation of this foundational sin has been sanctioned and even institutionalized by society. Many of us must confront the fact that, without necessarily choosing to do so, such biases have powerfully impacted and informed our attitudes, words and actions. We often do not even identify it with sin – it seems so subtle and acceptable. Yet it is absolutely contrary to God's view of His creation and the love He has for each specific aspect of it. Physical characteristics, including skin color and ethnic body variations, reflect His amazingly creative and beautiful wisdom and sovereignty. Our human uniqenesses and variations reflect (as do all other aspects of His creation) the fullness of the Lord. We individually and collectively as the entire human race exist and represent Him as His image bearers. Human differences and variation should bring Him glory and prompt us toward thanksgiving and praise. Yet in our fallen state men try to rule over other men in an effort to be "gods." In this way, once again, we reject being subject to the only true Creator God. The criteria the world employs as to who is superior to another often separates along social, economic or racial-ethnic criteria. Historically those who have the greatest power (to destroy or subject) select themselves as superior – they obtain, enjoy and flaunt social and economic world privilege. The race or ethnicity of the conquerors then is associated with superiority; other subjected races or ethnicities are then identified as inferior and to be treated with a lesser degree of respect and honor. A "master and slave" mentality can then emerge. We must always keep in mind that, at its root, racial discrimination is due to the most fundamental and determinative sin: pride and self-exaltation.

During the decades in which I was raised in America there were (as I now look back) overt and cruel prejudices embraced toward a variety of "minorities" (a term meaning those not holding power). They permeated all aspects of life: where one lives, jobs available, educational opportunities, relationship possibilities, leisure activities, the presence of criminal pressures, amount of material possessions and religious segregation. Along with these more external manifestations, people defined as minorities experienced and accepted an internal sense of devaluation and a negative self-regard. Spiritually, those who are devalued by society felt unworthy and forgotten by God.

Without my awareness or conscious choice, I was indoctrinated in and adopted a world view of social, ethnic and racial bias. Only as I came to see this issue through the lens of my growing identity in Christ and the truth of His Word, was I able to begin to see clearly my depravity in this area. Our modern emerging society is now reflecting an increasing intolerance toward prejudice and discrimination; this has also helped me to bring into question the beliefs and views of what previously had been imprinted into my person. Although much of modern society has, to our detriment, highlighted and glorified the depravity of the flesh, I believe, for our benefit, it has been helpful to uncover long accepted prejudices and bring forth a healthier view of how we regard others. As I have confronted my own background relative to this issue, I had to face a mixture of feelings and address a new set of questions with a variety of potential responses. I felt sadness, guilt, betrayal, and confusion. I feared that I would not know how to respond in a way that would not additionally offend. I struggled with why and how I arrived at adulthood with these ungodly views of my fellow man; how I should go about understanding more fully the issues and plight of those hurt by the years of discrimination; what active steps I should take to love those who have been marginalized or suppressed; and how to best invite people I had previously disregarded into my life. I wanted to know those who I had been subtlety taught to avoid and reject, and I longed to have them as friends. But I didn't know how to even begin, and I worried that the brewing anger and resentment in them would lash out against me in my uninformed and insensitive efforts. That's where I find myself now in these latter years.

How then would I advise you? Firstly, come face to face with the reality of this situation in your community; confront in truth your personal views of minorities and those who are and have been discriminated against. Be honest; expect internal pain and a variety of conflicting emotions. Secondly, take it to God, wrestle with Him on this, seek Biblical truth to guide you and ask for transformation by His Spirit. Thirdly, begin a dialogue and spend time with people who you have, in the past, not associated with because of class or race. Listen to them and try to empathize with their journey and their plight. You may find yourself becoming defensive and protective as you hear the truth; try to receive their words and feelings as their honest but often raw view of their journey. Although their hurt is not specifically against you personally, you may be regarded as a representative of the offenders. Fourthly, apologize and ask for forgiveness. Don't try to justify anything but accept your part in a corporate culpability. Fifthly, work hard to fight for them and move your community and country to the place that reflects God's desire for His creation. Finally, be willing to personally and sacrificially take a stand on this issue; speak and act in a radical and potentially counter-cultural manner. Be willing to feel judged by the "old guard" even to the point of rejection.

I urge you to be intentional and undaunted in your growth and maturation in this important area. You are a child of God and must let this reality shed light in all the dark recesses of your life.

Love,
David

Questions

Obviously in normal life one does not have the advantage to be able to evaluate and direct their life choices with the knowledge of their future. However, the author has in these letters created such a context to press each of us to focus on specific "life issues" proactively and intentionally in our younger years so that we, as we go forward, can direct our lives toward the best of all outcomes. These general questions should be regarded as a guide for the reader, individually or as a part of a small group, to address the issue at hand and make appropriate life decisions and choices.

What is the specific "life issue" the author is concerned about in this letter?

Why does the author feel this is an important issue to bring to a person's attention in their younger years; do you agree?

How did the author seem to deal with it as a younger man? Was his means of addressing the issue done properly or improperly, consciously or subconsciously, constructively or destructively, God honoring or man honoring?

How is the author, now as an older man, recommending that the specific issue be thought about and actively addressed?

The goal of each letter is not to convince the reader to deal with the issue as the author had, but to embrace the issue and determine for themselves how they choose to regard and deal with it in their lives.

Do you agree with the author's analyses and recommended manner of addressing it?

If so, explain how you will apply it in your specific life's circumstances.

If not, please elaborate on how you view the issue and how you plan to address it as you live out the rest of your life.

What wisdom would you desire your children to receive from you on this issue to better prepare and equip them to deal with it in a truthful and God-honoring manner?

Civic and Government Affairs

Letter 28

Romans 13:1-7

¹Let everyone be subject to the governing authorities, for there is no authority except that which God has established. The authorities that exist have been established by God. ² Consequently, whoever rebels against the authority is rebelling against what God has instituted, and those who do so will bring judgment on themselves. ³ For rulers hold no terror for those who do right, but for those who do wrong. Do you want to be free from fear of the one in authority? Then do what is right and you will be commended. ⁴ For the one in authority is God's servant for your good. But if you do wrong, be afraid, for rulers do not bear the sword for no reason. They are God's servants, agents of wrath to bring punishment on the wrongdoer. ⁵ Therefore, it is necessary to submit to the authorities, not only because of possible punishment but also as a matter of conscience.
⁶ This is also why you pay taxes, for the authorities are God's servants, who give their full time to governing. ⁷ Give to everyone what you owe them: If you owe taxes, pay taxes; if revenue, then revenue; if respect, then respect; if honor, then honor.

Dear David,

There are certain subjects, that I recognize and admit, in which I am not well versed – at least from man's perspective. My interest in and involvement with civic or government affairs has been meager and minimal. So, my thoughts in this letter are from the perspective of a citizen of the Kingdom of God who must reside in this broken and chaotic world. The goal of the ruler of this world, Satan, is to perpetuate chaos and facilitate the progressive destruction of God's creation. He rules this world, however, through people; because of our fallen state, all men are frail, influenceable and vulnerable, therefore, easily manipulated by Satan. It is important that you, David, understand the place and role of civil authority and human governance. It exists and has its power only because of God's wisdom and permissive will. Yet God is integrally involved in this level of human existence; He has, and will, superintend all of human history.

The net effect of the "fall" (as I have previously written about) is that every person views themselves as their own god and seeks to live in such a way as to fulfill their needs and desires. They will, overtly or covertly, obviously or subtly, by intent or habit, live to achieve their individual kingdom goals, despite and at the expense of another. Judges 21:25 describes the condition of fallen man: "…. everyone did as he saw fit." (Please bear in mind as I write this, I am describing the unrepentant and untransformed person and not those who have died in Christ and now live in Christ. Redeemed people can progressively live as children of the true King under His spiritual authority and governance.) If this collective self-seeking condition was not powerfully addressed by the sovereign God, the whole of mankind would live in anarchy and chaos; there would be overt, intentional and wholesale destruction of life.

God in His amazing wisdom and grace has mercifully permitted the establishment of governments and authorities in each culture (there are a variety of forms of governance) to keep a semblance of peace and order and to protect one person from another (individually, or in defined groups such as families or ethnic communities.) God has equipped government with the authority and power to make and uphold laws, establish means to meet societal needs, keep each person accountable to a level of conduct that permits necessary security, and to punish those whose self-interests violates the needs of civilization.

God will provide for and maintain in their place of power those persons or nations who fulfill properly the role He has allowed them. When such people or nations abuse or corrupt this God-given responsibility and privilege, He will (and has in history) remove His permissive will for them; they will lose their power and authority and their governance and structures will be destroyed or de-constructed. The governments that cooperate (intentionally or, more usually, coincidentally) with their God given responsibility and reflect to a sufficient extent His ethic will prosper and continue. Such cooperation will be evidenced in the ability of the people living under this government to know human security and material sufficiency. (Unless one is truly "in Christ" and lives under His reign, they cannot know true soulful peace, joy and abundance). Christians in authority can serve God more consistently and prosper the people they rule to a greater degree than those who reject His sovereign will in their lives. However, the enemy and ruler of the world knows this and will do everything possible to "dethrone" godly Christians from government.

The responsibility of each Christian and every Christian family is to accept the authority above them and comply with the rules, laws and expectations of the government (see Romans 13:1-7 and 1 Peter 2:13-25). Anarchy and rebellion, law-breaking and civil disobedience, criminal and destructive behaviors should not be a part of the godly person's life choices; they should, in fact, oppose such whenever possible. The believer should pray constantly that their leaders resist their flesh desires and the influence of Satan; they should pray that these leaders seek to do their work in an honest and trustworthy manner, being accountable to others in authority and the populous in general (see 1 Timothy 2:1-2). Although we would ideally want them to know God and seek His wisdom and will, we should, even if they don't seek God, pray for their guidance and protection, and that God, through their efforts and wise choices, will keep men at peace. David, I believe that God will not allow man to destroy His created world (including mankind) and will intervene to allow nations to exist and survive until He chooses to return (Second Advent). Then and only then will all things be judged, evil destroyed and the new world (perfectly restored) established. Then Christ will govern as King with complete and perfect righteousness and justice. God will allow this world, broken as it is, to exist until the Gospel has been announced to the whole of mankind and all will have had opportunity to hear and respond.

As a note-worthy comment, the "Arab-Israeli" conflict will never be resolved and there will never be a victor until God's plan for the world is completed and all Biblical prophesies fulfilled. The balance of power will ebb and flow, rise and fall, bounce back and forth from one side to the other but until His time is at hand there will be no lasting peace or resolution. Other nations will align with one or the other in this eternal conflict in order to maintain balance, awaiting His definitive action. This conflict has arisen out of the spiritual warfare that surrounds God's plan of salvation; it has been and will continue to permeate and influence all of human history.

I end with a caveat, one that I write with trepidation for fear that it be misapplied or misused. If it is clear that what is being asked from the authorities is in direct opposition to God's specific will, as confirmed by Scripture and the unanimous view of all godly people concerned, then one can consider disobedience to the directive of the government. What is judged worthy of such disobedience must be that which, if followed, would be destructive to the Kingdom of God, and by complying with it we would disgrace Christ and our identity in Him and counter the necessary work of showing Christ to the hurting world. To disobey authority, however, may require you to be willing to accept the consequences of this stance: suffering, persecution and even martyrdom. God, I must remind you, rarely asks this of His children, but if led to choose this stance, we must be willing to die for Him and His Kingdom. Of course, Christ is the ultimate example and embodiment of this situation (a modern-day example could be Dietrich Bonhoeffer).

David, obey the laws, be a good citizen and vote responsibly; live your life in this light and with this perspective; teach it to your daughters.

Love,
David

Questions

Obviously in normal life one does not have the advantage to be able to evaluate and direct their life choices with the knowledge of their future. However, the author has in these letters created such a context to press each of us to focus on specific "life issues" proactively and intentionally in our younger years so that we, as we go forward, can direct our lives toward the best of all outcomes. These general questions should be regarded as a guide for the reader, individually or as a part of a small group, to address the issue at hand and make appropriate life decisions and choices.

What is the specific "life issue" the author is concerned about in this letter?

Why does the author feel this is an important issue to bring to a person's attention in their younger years; do you agree?

How did the author seem to deal with it as a younger man? Was his means of addressing the issue done properly or improperly, consciously or subconsciously, constructively or destructively, God honoring or man honoring?

How is the author, now as an older man, recommending that the specific issue be thought about and actively addressed?

The goal of each letter is not to convince the reader to deal with the issue as the author had, but to embrace the issue and determine for themselves how they choose to regard and deal with it in their lives.

Do you agree with the author's analyses and recommended manner of addressing it?

If so, explain how you will apply it in your specific life's circumstances.

If not, please elaborate on how you view the issue and how you plan to address it as you live out the rest of your life.

What wisdom would you desire your children to receive from you on this issue to better prepare and equip them to deal with it in a truthful and God-honoring manner?

The Problem of Evil

Letter 29

Ephesians 6:12-13

12 For our struggle is not against flesh and blood, but against the rulers, against the authorities, against the powers of this dark world and against the spiritual forces of evil in the heavenly realms. 13 Therefore put on the full armor of God, so that when the day of evil comes, you may be able to stand your ground, and after you have done everything, to stand.

James 1:13-15

13 When tempted, no one should say, "God is tempting me." For God cannot be tempted by evil, nor does he tempt anyone; 14 but each person is tempted when they are dragged away by their own evil desire and enticed. 15 Then, after desire has conceived, it gives birth to sin; and sin, when it is full-grown, gives birth to death.

Dear David,

The overall purpose for writing these letters to you is to benefit you, perhaps, with wisdom gained through years of living. They are intended to avail you of what I have come to see as right, good, worthy or important so that you might actively address these chosen topics in your life as you go forward. Many of the topics addressed are practical and are applicable to life choices; they urge or call for a pragmatic, intentional action.

The issue I will confront you with in this letter is not directly implementable or action directed. Although I debated in my mind about whether I should address it or not, my spirit has been urging me to do so; so, I shall. Even though it is by its nature less practical, I believe it is an important concept to wrestle with because it can formulate or alter how you view occurrences or experiences in life that seek to challenge your view of and faith in God. The issue I will address is the issue of evil; I shall attempt to confront the question of why there is such pain, suffering or oppression in life, even for the person walking with God!

This issue is a complex and multifaceted one; it should be understood primarily from a spiritual perspective. If we try to make sense of it by our human reasoning or from an ethical humanistic perspective, we will be confused and find ourselves overwhelmed with a sense of despair or anger; it will press us toward agnosticism.

You first must recall and firmly ground yourself upon the Biblical truth that informs our mind with what God had intended for creation, mankind being the pinnacle of it. His creation (biblically termed the "Garden of Eden"), before Adam and Eve arrogantly disobeyed God, was a perfect world without pain, illness, turmoil, suffering, persecution or oppression. Physically, emotionally and relationally (in our interactions with God and all other aspects of His creation) we were created to enjoy this perfection. His intention was that as long as people allowed Him to be their God, they would know complete joy and peace. At the same time God knew through divine wisdom, even before creation, that mankind (and through man, all creation) would succumb to original sin: wanting to be each their own god. Parenthetically, keep in mind that we are promised that after Christ's second return and the complete annihilation of sin (including Satan) eternal life will be enjoyed in the restored world, once again made perfect as He intended.

This rejection of God's proper place in His world and, instead, choosing to be our own god brought a rapid estrangement from God and a conflictual division between man and all the rest of God's creation (animal, vegetable and natural forces). Relationships between one person and another became divisive, dishonest, suspicious, and aggressive. Every person's words and actions sought to exalt themselves at the expense of everything and everyone else. War, slavery, genocide, prejudices, torture and the like became the way of mankind. Fear and anxiety characterized man's daily life. Animals became enemies to one another and to man; many parts of the vegetation differentiated into toxic, poisonous and pain inflicted agents, and the imbalance of a cosmos where God is longer in control, brought forth a variety of natural disasters. It was man's choice to dislodge the creation from the control of the creator and thereby thrusting all things of creation into a state of "imbalance" leading progressively toward destruction – a relentlessly painful journey. Man now lives by a fallen flesh nature in a fallen world.

This "sin driven and sin saturated world" that creation was catapulted into by man's rejection of his created role was further added to by two additional and powerful realities. The first of these realities is that God, clearly and fully aware of this situation, had to respond in a manner befitting and reflecting His perfect character: a character of righteousness that demands justice. For Him to have not responded with judgement would have compromised His character and He would not be fully God – this is impossible. He is God and therefore He must and will act like God. According to His just character, then, He declares to mankind that in various ways they will forever (until Christ provides the necessary solution) know the pain and difficulty of surviving in this now fallen and depraved world, even as they bear their children (see Genesis 3:14-19). These "curses" (actually earned and deserved judgements and punishments) are now added to the sufferings of the flesh nature of man described above. I often hear from Christ skeptics that: "If God is love, how can He stand by and allow such suffering in this world"?! God certainly is love, He defines and personifies love, but He is also a God of perfect justice and is righteous in every way. From the time of the fall until He establishes His restored creation and all forces of evil and our flesh nature have been annihilated, He holds love and justice in tension. He creatively offers and pours out His love upon those who are His followers (by virtue of trust in God's plan of salvation through Christ) as they must continue to live in this current broken world. Now as we live in the "Spiritual Kingdom of God" (after Christ's first advent and resurrection) the Holy Spirit administers this love and the wisdom needed to survive and prosper. His presence through the Spirit indwells our present suffering and persecutions, so that we are strengthened and enabled to serve Him in this present spiritual kingdom. Those who are not His followers do not have access to this love and wisdom, through the Spirit, and feel only the pain of living in this depraved world. Now as we live as Christians in this fallen world, we await in absolute confidence ("hope") for His final advent and the defeat of all that had caused our suffering. While we wait, we endure and serve, guided and empowered by His love, provision and protection.

The second reality added to the fallen nature of all creation is that of the active and powerful presence and work of Satan. To deny his existence and his involvement in the affairs of the now fallen world is to walk in blindness (no "spiritual sight") and to be an easy target for Satan as he intercedes in our life. He seeks to entice and direct our flesh nature to live as depraved people in our sin, apart from God (James 1:13-15; Ephesians 6:12-13, 1 Peter 5:8-9). You can easily observe him doing this in the lives of the vast majority of people who live apart from God, and especially in those who hold the power in this world. He encourages chaos, injustice, cruelty, prejudice, hate, violence and self-exaltation, to name a few. Satan is proactive, intentional and much more powerful than men. He is angry and motivated by a sense of urgency because he knows he has been defeated by Christ on the cross and his time of destructive control is short. He is acting feverishly to destroy the lives of many people and rob them of eternity before Christ returns and he is completely annihilated.

When people are hurting, I often hear them questioning why God is allowing or causing them personally to suffer!? They ask what they did wrong to cause God to put them in that position. They either see themselves as the cause of their painful situation or they conclude that God is impotent, uncaring or non-existent. They grapple with these thoughts because they never were really told the truth concerning evil and Satan. God did not (He cannot according to His character) cause their specific and present suffering. Further Jesus is clear in His teaching that pain and suffering are common to the lives of all of fallen creation, and one's specific situation is not due to their individual merit or demerit as a person (although our daily choices will bring consequences that can add additional pain and suffering). In these times we must come alongside of our hurting friends and explain to them these truths.

The good news, David, that you must keep in mind and represent to those you can influence, is that this time of pain and suffering is limited – it will be ended at Christ's second return. This situation was never God's intention but exists for a season by His permission so that all that would seek Him and His plan for salvation will hear the "good news" and be able to enter someday the restored creation, Heaven.

As you now better understand the complexity and multiple factors involved in our human condition (that includes suffering), you will be better able to endure it, modify or change your daily life's choices and enhance your prayer life to address it. You must help others, especially your children, understand this issue so that they will not be discouraged and overwhelmed by the realities of human existence. Although difficult, you and they must seek God more intentionally during times of pain and thank Him for these unique opportunities to grow in faith and knowledge of Him.

Love,
David

Questions

Obviously in normal life one does not have the advantage to be able to evaluate and direct their life choices with the knowledge of their future. However, the author has in these letters created such a context to press each of us to focus on specific "life issues" proactively and intentionally in our younger years so that we, as we go forward, can direct our lives toward the best of all outcomes. These general questions should be regarded as a guide for the reader, individually or as a part of a small group, to address the issue at hand and make appropriate life decisions and choices.

What is the specific "life issue" the author is concerned about in this letter?

Why does the author feel this is an important issue to bring to a person's attention in their younger years; do you agree?

How did the author seem to deal with it as a younger man? Was his means of addressing the issue done properly or improperly, consciously or subconsciously, constructively or destructively, God honoring or man honoring?

How is the author, now as an older man, recommending that the specific issue be thought about and actively addressed?

The goal of each letter is not to convince the reader to deal with the issue as the author had, but to embrace the issue and determine for themselves how they choose to regard and deal with it in their lives.

Do you agree with the author's analyses and recommended manner of addressing it?

If so, explain how you will apply it in your specific life's circumstances.

If not, please elaborate on how you view the issue and how you plan to address it as you live out the rest of your life.

What wisdom would you desire your children to receive from you on this issue to better prepare and equip them to deal with it in a truthful and God-honoring manner?

The Fight
Letter 30

1 Peter 5:8
8 Be alert and of sober mind. Your enemy the devil prowls around like a roaring lion looking for someone to devour.

Ephesians 5:15
15 Be very careful, then, how you live—not as unwise but as wise,

Dear David,

I need to alert and prepare you for a reality that you will deal with almost daily for your entire life. It is an unhappy reality that is frequently accompanied by pain, anxiety, grief and disappointment. Although very real, most people go through life unaware of it, or if vaguely aware of it, do not take it seriously. We are deceived when we do not understand and accept as truth that we, especially as Christ followers, are daily in battle with spiritual forces that are way smarter, more creative and powerful than ourselves. These contrary spiritual forces can be enmeshed and hidden within our relationships with other people, natural events, life's circumstances and our own flesh nature. I believe it is best to think of life as an ongoing fight; a fight that if fought in our human ability and strength will be lost.

As I wrote in the previous letter, evil is present and powerful in this fallen world as a part of human existence; it rules the "kingdom of the world." Yet we generally are not made aware of this, as we grow up, by parents or teachers, in our homes or schools. We are taught and come to believe that if we understand and cooperate with the world's ways, make good and right choices in life, know and relate to the "right people" and have a bit of good luck, we will at some point come to enjoy a comfortable existence. We foolishly and irrationally believe that "tomorrow" everything will fall into place and come together for our benefit and enjoyment. We think that if we can just get over this present hurdle, all will be fine. We conduct our life with thoughts like: "If I can just learn to ride a bicycle, or make the football team or cheerleading squad, or get into that college, or find the right spouse, or get that high paying job, or have that sports car, or retire to play golf and move to Florida then life will be good!" These and any number of other deceptive goals that people believe will bring them happiness are embraced and frantically pursued. Yet the reality is that spiritual forces are continually at work to deceive you in this; they taint, sabotage, dilute or disappoint you in your efforts to reach this human and worldly endorsed goal. The result will certainly be an unsatisfying outcome. Creatively, and often unexpectantly, something or someone inevitably interferes or complicates what you are expecting to happen. Or, after you finally achieve or acquire that which the world encourages as a goal, you are left feeling empty and betrayed; this often occurring right on the heels of and spoiling your "celebration of achievement." A powerfully negative word or act robs you of your "moment of glory." I am always amazed and sadly impressed with how ingenious and creatively clever evil plays out its role as we live in this world. Yet rarely does anyone acknowledge this certain reality and live their life in expectation and proper preparedness for it. People live life in the deceptive fantasy that there is no spiritual war and we are not in a fight.

It is important, David, that you understand this now, prepare properly for it, and inform intentionally your daughters of it. The good news, though, is that you need not fight this fight yourself, although Satan (the ruler of the kingdom of the world) would have you believe you can. His two primary tools against us are, firstly, to blind you to the reality of the fight and secondly, even if you accept that there is a fight, he will convince you that you can prevail by your human efforts alone. As a follower of Christ, you have His powerful and even more creative (than Satan) resources to call upon in every skirmish or major battle you will find yourself in throughout your life. You must strive to know God and appropriate the promises He has made to you, His child, that flow out of His love. In a daily life of confession, repentance and humbly seeking after Him, you will know true peace and joy. Such peace and joy are the true fruit of the victory in the fight we participate in daily. Do not misunderstand me; you will know pain, grief, disappointment and all other forms of painful human emotions. Our faith does not protect us from the distress of living in a fallen world. That is not the criteria that defines our victory in this fight. Our victory is that in the midst of the fight, God is with us and we experience His comfort, peace and joy, despite the pain of the world. We are able to come to know a higher and deeply satisfying reality as we live a life flowing out of that living relationship with Him. No matter what "slings and arrows" the enemy throws our way, God will, as we allow Him, bring victory.

Please be forewarned and live a life of prepared combat using the full armor of God (Ephesians 6:10-18). Jesus has secured the ultimate victory, but we are engaged in daily battles for as long as we live. Bring His wisdom and power into your fight.

I love you,
David

Questions

Obviously in normal life one does not have the advantage to be able to evaluate and direct their life choices with the knowledge of their future. However, the author has in these letters created such a context to press each of us to focus on specific "life issues" proactively and intentionally in our younger years so that we, as we go forward, can direct our lives toward the best of all outcomes. These general questions should be regarded as a guide for the reader, individually or as a part of a small group, to address the issue at hand and make appropriate life decisions and choices.

What is the specific "life issue" the author is concerned about in this letter?

Why does the author feel this is an important issue to bring to a person's attention in their younger years; do you agree?

How did the author seem to deal with it as a younger man? Was his means of addressing the issue done properly or improperly, consciously or subconsciously, constructively or destructively, God honoring or man honoring?

How is the author, now as an older man, recommending that the specific issue be thought about and actively addressed?

The goal of each letter is not to convince the reader to deal with the issue as the author had, but to embrace the issue and determine for themselves how they choose to regard and deal with it in their lives.

Do you agree with the author's analyses and recommended manner of addressing it?

If so, explain how you will apply it in your specific life's circumstances.

If not, please elaborate on how you view the issue and how you plan to address it as you live out the rest of your life.

What wisdom would you desire your children to receive from you on this issue to better prepare and equip them to deal with it in a truthful and God-honoring manner?

Midlife Challenges
Letter 31

Philippians 3:8-9
[8] What is more, I consider everything a loss because of the surpassing worth of knowing Christ Jesus my Lord, for whose sake I have lost all things. I consider them garbage, that I may gain Christ [9] and be found in him, not having a righteousness of my own that comes from the law, but that which is through faith in Christ—the righteousness that comes from God on the basis of faith.

Matthew 11:28-29
[28] "Come to me, all you who are weary and burdened, and I will give you rest. [29] Take my yoke upon you and learn from me, for I am gentle and humble in heart, and you will find rest for your souls.

Dear David,

I realize that I am writing to you as you are in the midst of the most productive, active and confident years of your adult life. Your career is escalating; you are acquiring life's possessions; you are developing rewarding relationships; you are growing in intimacy with Judy (exploring together life's opportunities); you are rising to levels of leadership and influence in the local church and you are experiencing the rewarding complexities of fatherhood. Although tumultuous and very busy, you feel secure, confident and "in control." It is, in many ways, a great time of your life.

I must though, in this letter, prepare you for the next stage of your life, so that you can negotiate it without making regrettable mistakes that will impact not only yourself and your whole family, but also, most importantly, your potential service in the Kingdom. I speak of the "midlife challenges" that must be navigated properly so that they do not become "crises" that could threaten to destroy that which God has begun (Philippians 1:6). Many men deal with their failures in this life's stage after it goes wrong and then from a perspective of needing to remediate significant mistakes. My hope is to prevent you from being personally damaged in this difficult crucible of life.

There are probably a variety of factors that lead to the thoughts and feelings people experience in the middle adult years: personality, previous "semi-wrong" choices, poor modeling, the changing appearance of the body and their hormones, disappointment in level of achievement and success, a perceived lack of happiness or "fulfillment," rocky marital and family relationships and the stress-fatigue state that has resulted from an overly ambitious and carelessly pursued young adult life. However, I believe there is a crucial spiritual component to this as well. The self-sufficiency, prideful self-confidence, and arrogantly independent trust in our human strength and ability sets one up to, sooner or later, encounter that which causes them to fail painfully; they then find themselves in a broken and disappointed state. Satan, aware of this human flesh tendency and the traps of

155

midlife, will utilize these ego driven ways to cause a person to make decisions that can lead to destruction at a variety of levels.

As you navigate through these midlife challenges and the emotional and relational assaults they produce, you could find yourself gradually becoming desensitized to and rationalizing away your previously held Biblical moral code and choosing to enact, little-by-little, unwise and not God-pleasing decisions. You will, in an effort to avoid a sense of guilt and self-condemnation, remove yourself from the godly wisdom and advice of other spiritually strong people and turn away from the Bible; you might trade your previously held relational Christianity for a hollow religious obligation. You may begin to feel angry about or pity yourself for your unsatisfying life situation; you may begin to commiserate with other men who are moving with you along this trajectory. You might consider, even frantically at times, becoming involved in the things of the world or of the flesh that will feed your ego and give you sensual pleasure. You may give more time to your leisure and hobbies, and less time to the family; you may choose to throw yourself full throttle into your profession. You may choose to vigorously exercise in order to hold onto your youth; you may change your appearance or your style of dress to be more attractive to others and to your declining self-image. Marital infidelity might now seem justified and permissible. All these potential choices are designed to regain what you have perceived as lost: pleasure, acknowledgment, appreciation and the "pizazz of life!" Although all this can happen with your awareness, you rationalize them as being beneficial and necessary and refuse to acknowledge such decisions as detrimental directions. If you do not put the brakes on this "slide" you stand to risk ultimately losing your marriage, family, friends (previously loyal), financial security and the esteem of others (community and church). Your career may be also negatively impacted, or, in the worst case, you will choose to jettison your profession and feverishly seek "something else" – but you are at a loss as to what.

You must be alert and prepared to recognize and address these features of the midlife years; they can creep in insidiously and rise within you like yeast in flour (Biblical agent of evil). Stay open, honest and transparent with your wife; seek to develop a deep and strong disciplining relationship with a mature Christian man in which you can be candid and accountable; stay in the Word and escalate your prayer life – asking God's help and protection. Seek out and enact appropriate changes (in collaboration with your wife) for yourself and your life: appearance, career, interests, goals, vacations and opportunities. For example, I bought myself an MG-TD and restored it as a way to "treat myself" and introduce an element of excitement. Suggest, lovingly and sensitively, changes others, especially your wife, could make to help you; realize she can't be "21" again and has to care for the responsibilities of her life as well. Seek solid Christian counselling and be open to the need for medications. Do not reject your tried and true friends, but instead be open to their involvement and assistance in your journey. In general, try to avoid making any major decisions during this time; in all likelihood they will be poor choices and will cause havoc and destruction to multiple lives. You are not able to think clearly and will regret decisions made in this vulnerable and myopic state.

I can assure you that if you remain close to God and use the suggestions above you will weather this problematic and potentially destructive stage in your life. You will grow stronger in the process and can become even more secure and productive in the Kingdom.

Love, David

Questions

Obviously in normal life one does not have the advantage to be able to evaluate and direct their life choices with the knowledge of their future. However, the author has in these letters created such a context to press each of us to focus on specific "life issues" proactively and intentionally in our younger years so that we, as we go forward, can direct our lives toward the best of all outcomes. These general questions should be regarded as a guide for the reader, individually or as a part of a small group, to address the issue at hand and make appropriate life decisions and choices.

What is the specific "life issue" the author is concerned about in this letter?

Why does the author feel this is an important issue to bring to a person's attention in their younger years; do you agree?

How did the author seem to deal with it as a younger man? Was his means of addressing the issue done properly or improperly, consciously or subconsciously, constructively or destructively, God honoring or man honoring?

How is the author, now as an older man, recommending that the specific issue be thought about and actively addressed?

The goal of each letter is not to convince the reader to deal with the issue as the author had, but to embrace the issue and determine for themselves how they choose to regard and deal with it in their lives.

Do you agree with the author's analyses and recommended manner of addressing it?

If so, explain how you will apply it in your specific life's circumstances.

If not, please elaborate on how you view the issue and how you plan to address it as you live out the rest of your life.

What wisdom would you desire your children to receive from you on this issue to better prepare and equip them to deal with it in a truthful and God-honoring manner?

The Wasted Wisdom of the Elderly

Letter 32

Psalm 92:14
14 They will still bear fruit in old age, they will stay fresh and green.
Acts 20:24
24 However, I consider my life worth nothing to me; my only aim is to finish the race and complete the task the Lord Jesus has given me—the task of testifying to the good news of God's grace.

Dear David,

This letter will distinguish itself from the others because it is addressing an issue that I am currently dealing with. Since I am still exploring and trying to find my way in this, the wisdom I offer is partial and unproven in my life. Yet I do feel I have sufficient insight into it, based on my journey so far and the journey I know about from others further along, such that I can offer thoughts for your consideration. As always, the goal of this letter is to prepare you now for what will come so that you can address and navigate the concern better than I, and most others, have done. The topic I shall address is that of the "elder years" – that time when our bodies and minds are experiencing the effect of age and when society's view of what we can contribute has a distinctive flavor. I also refer you to letter 33 on "Ownership and Control," when I elaborate on achieving peaceful aging.

Sadly, as I look around and pay attention to this area in our American culture, I see people of age being marginalized and trivialized. They are often seen as non-contributory, dependent and resource consumers. Many families struggle to know how to properly regard their aging kinfolk while they carry on their full younger lives. Although they may love the elder member of the extended family, they (without openly acknowledging, or even being aware) do not let the perspectives, opinions and advice of the elder direct or impact their daily lives. The concept of "the wisdom of age" has been extinguished in modern Western society. This situation, I believe, has arisen due to the failure on the part of both parties: the elder (individually and as a societal entity) and the younger generation. I acknowledge there is variability as to how different families deal with this issue and that my comments are generalizations.

Let me first begin with some thoughts and directives to the aged person relative to their role in this dynamic. The older person often arrives at this stage in their life having not lived their life in a manner that has established them as worthy of respect, honor and as a source of wisdom. They should be established as persons of integrity, wisdom, reasonableness and patience; they should be regarded as one who listens well and is not judgmental. They should display a refreshing transparency and openness to deep sharing. The life they have lived, as evaluated by their family and others, should be viewed as valuable and exemplary. The relationship they have, and have had, with their spouse should be one that is characterized as deeply caring, intimate and materially sufficient to provide for each other. The elderly couple who is able to function as a contributing and mutually edifying unit is a beautiful model and example for the youth to behold. Further, it is essential for them, over their younger years, to have chosen to invest time and effort into establishing and maintaining a relationship with their children and grandchildren.

The aged person must refuse to accept that they are not able to contribute or be effective in their influence. If they relinquish this belief in themselves and their abilities, society and the younger generation will quickly accept their resignation and take over, and in doing so confirm the non-essential and impotent role of the aged person. If one is able and capable of contributing, then they must, and not allow themselves to be regarded otherwise. They must believe that they have knowledge and experience that would be of great benefit for younger people. Yet it is important that this confidence be tempered by a humble spirit so that they are not viewed as imposing themselves on others. They also must realize that they likely will not be fully aware of the idiosyncrasies and ways of the younger generation. They should also be seen as a person who is still teachable and continually growing in their knowledge and understanding of life and of God. A more tangible but valuable aspect of the Senior is their ability to contribute material resources and finances; the older person should distinguish themselves as being generous. The benefit to society and particularly God's Kingdom's work can be substantially furthered by such resource allocation. Finally, the senior must continue (they should have been seeking this all their life) to stay physically strong and healthy, and mentally sharp. Of course, there are the inevitable effects of time, genetics and illness that will modify or deny their ability and desire to accomplish this goal.

Let me now turn to the younger generation who must also reevaluate and alter their view of and regard for the elderly. I have seen, sadly, cases where an aged person, who is strong, knowledgeable, capable, secure and vibrant, has been ignored or disregarded simply due to their age. Too infrequently do younger people seek out the counsel and wisdom of the senior; they feel that their peers rather than the older person hold desired truths and insights. Obviously, such a perspective will significantly rob the world of valuable experience and proven, mature and rich counsel. We will be "re-inventing the wheel" with each successive generation. The younger generation needs to be educated as to what the older generation can offer and make an active decision to honestly seek out these contributions. One of the most tragic applications of their disregard is in the area of our local church. The spiritual and Biblical richness of those who have lived longer and fellowshipped deeply with the Lord during their life's journey is an enormously valuable asset for God's household. Yet churches regularly focus on the youth and use the young as their leaders.

With this being said, I exhort you, David, to do what you can to change this counter-productive and tragic state. I exhort you to find those older people in your environment (even within your extended family) that can and will speak into you and your family's life. Admittedly however we cannot quickly change society and its corporate disregard for the aged person. Also show your daughters how to appreciate and utilize the amazing and valuable resources of the elder person.

Love,
David

Questions

Obviously in normal life one does not have the advantage to be able to evaluate and direct their life choices with the knowledge of their future. However, the author has in these letters created such a context to press each of us to focus on specific "life issues" proactively and intentionally in our younger years so that we, as we go forward, can direct our lives toward the best of all outcomes. These general questions should be regarded as a guide for the reader, individually or as a part of a small group, to address the issue at hand and make appropriate life decisions and choices.

What is the specific "life issue" the author is concerned about in this letter?

Why does the author feel this is an important issue to bring to a person's attention in their younger years; do you agree?

How did the author seem to deal with it as a younger man? Was his means of addressing the issue done properly or improperly, consciously or subconsciously, constructively or destructively, God honoring or man honoring?

How is the author, now as an older man, recommending that the specific issue be thought about and actively addressed?

The goal of each letter is not to convince the reader to deal with the issue as the author had, but to embrace the issue and determine for themselves how they choose to regard and deal with it in their lives.

Do you agree with the author's analyses and recommended manner of addressing it?

If so, explain how you will apply it in your specific life's circumstances.

If not, please elaborate on how you view the issue and how you plan to address it as you live out the rest of your life.

What wisdom would you desire your children to receive from you on this issue to better prepare and equip them to deal with it in a truthful and God-honoring manner?

Ownership and Control
Letter 33

Romans 6:16-18
16 Don't you know that when you offer yourselves to someone as obedient slaves, you are slaves of the one you obey—whether you are slaves to sin, which leads to death, or to obedience, which leads to righteousness? 17 But thanks be to God that, though you used to be slaves to sin, you have come to obey from your heart the pattern of teaching that has now claimed your allegiance. 18 You have been set free from sin and have become slaves to righteousness.

1 Corinthians 6:19-20
19 Do you not know that your bodies are temples of the Holy Spirit, who is in you, whom you have received from God? You are not your own; 20 you were bought at a price. Therefore honor God with your bodies.

Dear David,

I shall begin this letter with again a reference to aging. The contents of this letter arise out of my years of life and having arrived at the age where I could be regarded as being "old." From this perspective, I now make this concluding statement: peaceful aging is being content with losing control of what you thought you owned. I know this sounds a bit unconventional (compared to the usual human perspective on aging) and, at first glance, a bit confusing. Let me explain further.

In this area, as is so many other areas of life, truth and true reality have been withheld or blinded to our awareness by the world's wisdom and ways. Most of us (myself included) were raised with the world-view that seeks acquisitions and ownership. We were taught to define ourselves by our wealth and possessions, and the power this gives us in the world. We sought to own toys, collections (i.e. "baseball cards" or dolls), clothes, homes, cars and numerous other things. If we could not own them, we sought, as if it were possible, to control or have charge over areas of our life, such as our health, our friends, our family, our work or our retirement life. Relationships, as well, were often viewed as the means of meeting one's self-serving needs. Bill Cosby (a comedian whose life became tainted by immorality) epitomized this control-ownership mentality on his TV series when he would tell his son: "I brought you into this world and I can take you out of it!" He implied that he owned his son and had complete control over his life. This world view of our ownership and control is deceptive and destructive; it's most damaging effect is to obscure and deny us of what constitutes true life. True life comes from "denying self" and enacting sacrificial love, in seeking God's will and not ours, and in giving up our hold on this world and instead willingly emptying ourselves of it. Admittedly, such a view is counter-cultural and, from the world's perspective, irrational and foolish. We are led to believe it would deprive us of "the good things of life!"

In reality, we do not own or control what we think we do or can, but we are in fact a slave to this joy-robbing and death-enacting world philosophy. It controls us; it owns us. If you speak to people who have lived as the world has instructed, and they are able to be honest with themselves and you, they will testify that their life is, or was, a "house of cards." These so-called goals, priorities and achievements are seen in retrospect as temporary and transient, a superficial façade, and a source, in the end, of loneliness, fear, bitterness, resentment, anger and grief. It was, they now understood, a betrayal of true reality. They describe a feeling of being "double-crossed or let down." Inevitably, sooner or later, this house of cards will fall into a formless mess, valueless and unable to give life as it promised.

In the musical Les Misérables, the character Jean Valjean, as he beholds Colette, the young woman he raised from a child, embracing her future husband, Marius, made the poignant statement: "She was never mine to keep." He understood in that moment that even his daughter whom he loved sacrificially was not his to own, nor was he able to control her to do his bidding for his own needs. He was given the temporary job of raising her for God, but she was not his possession. There was a sense of grief because he had been mistaken all these years and now had to face what was always the truth, but he was blinded to it. Yet, there was also a sense of relief because, as he now understood, God was, and always had been, in control; he felt a fresh freedom as he could entrust her to God and feel confident that she would thrive and be secure. Peace and true joy in life was only possible for her and him (and all of us) when we come to this realization and understanding.

God alone owns and is thereby entitled to control that which He has created. One part of creation does not own or control another part, but only the creator has that privilege and responsibility. As we grow in our awareness of this truth and willingly give over our false façade of ownership and control to God, then an unequaled and unimaginable soulful joy and peace will be experienced. Our journey will, when directed by Him, be one of excitement, value and meaning. We will walk daily in trust and dependency upon Him, His will, His wisdom and His leading. He will give us new eyes and ears to see and hear what and how we are to experience His creation. He will instruct us in how to relate to Him as sovereign Lord of everything and as how to be His instruments of transformation in this world. We are, as Paul explains (Romans 6:15-23), now a slave to Him and righteousness and are no longer a slave to the destructive and death rending way of the world (a world built upon each of us seeking to be our own god). Jesus and Paul as they powerfully reach out to us from the words of the Bible are the greatest examples of relinquishing ownership and control. Sacrificial love (see 1 Cor. 13) is only possible as we are transformed by His Spirit from owners to being God owned, from controlling to being God controlled. This type of love is the greatest of all virtues; its power to give life to others is unique and unequalled. Yet, David, never worry or fear that living this new way will be at all negative, for when God owns and controls our lives, we will know blessings beyond all we could imagine. Our response then is one full of praise and gratefulness.

A gauge then, in my view, of how successfully we have lived our life as we enter these "aged years" is the degree of peace and contentedness we can experience as we relinquish control and ownership. It will take a lifetime to more fully understand and implement this truth but the earlier you begin the process and direct yourself to move along toward this goal, the longer you will enjoy true life and be able to serve God properly in His Kingdom.

Love, David

Questions

Obviously in normal life one does not have the advantage to be able to evaluate and direct their life choices with the knowledge of their future. However, the author has in these letters created such a context to press each of us to focus on specific "life issues" proactively and intentionally in our younger years so that we, as we go forward, can direct our lives toward the best of all outcomes. These general questions should be regarded as a guide for the reader, individually or as a part of a small group, to address the issue at hand and make appropriate life decisions and choices.

What is the specific "life issue" the author is concerned about in this letter?

Why does the author feel this is an important issue to bring to a person's attention in their younger years; do you agree?

How did the author seem to deal with it as a younger man? Was his means of addressing the issue done properly or improperly, consciously or subconsciously, constructively or destructively, God honoring or man honoring?

How is the author, now as an older man, recommending that the specific issue be thought about and actively addressed?

The goal of each letter is not to convince the reader to deal with the issue as the author had, but to embrace the issue and determine for themselves how they choose to regard and deal with it in their lives.

Do you agree with the author's analyses and recommended manner of addressing it?

If so, explain how you will apply it in your specific life's circumstances.

If not, please elaborate on how you view the issue and how you plan to address it as you live out the rest of your life.

What wisdom would you desire your children to receive from you on this issue to better prepare and equip them to deal with it in a truthful and God-honoring manner?